I have received no more

than one or two letters

in my life that were

worth the postage.

—*Henry David Thoreau*

P.S.
My Bush Pig's
Name is Boris

James C. Wade

CORGI BOOKS

for Rosine and Malcolm

JAMES C. WADE III

Case postale 103
Montchoisi,
1000 Lausanne 19
Switzerland

November 20, 1989

Reid's Hotel
Attn: the Manager
Funchal, Madeira
Portugal

Dear Sirs,

Do you accept animals in your hotel? I would be interested in a three-week stay in May of next year if my bush pigs could stay in an adjoining room.

I would appreciate your reply as soon as possible.

Sincerely yours,

[signature]

Reid's Hotel

★ ★ ★ ★ ★

Tel. (91) 23001 - Tlx. 72139 - Fax: (91) 30499 - Cables: Reidshotel

P – 9000 FUNCHAL - MADEIRA

PORTUGAL

Mr. James C. Wade III
Case postale 103
Montchoisi
1000 LAUSANNE 19
Switzerland

27th November, 1989

Dear Sir,

Thank you very much for your letter of 20th November the contents of which had our best attention.

We would very much appreciate if you could inform us what you really mean by "bush pigs" as we do not know that kind of animal. We do accept small dogs, but they are now allowed to be in public areas; such as Restaurants, Bars, Swimming-Pools and Salons.

Looking forward to hearing from you in order to give you a definitive answer in respect of your query, in the meantime, we remain,

Yours faithfully
REID'S HOTEL

D.A. Margeridon
Deputy General Manager

DM/MGTS

ISLAND HOTEL (MADEIRA) LTD.
Registered Office: Beckett House, 1 Lambeth Palace Road, London SE1 7EU
Company N.° England 328212, N.° Ind. P. Colectiva 500878897

JAMES C. WADE III

Case postale 103
Montchoisi
1000 Lausanne 19
Switzerland

December 6, 1989

Reid's Hotel
Attn: Mr. D. A. Margeridon,
Deputy General Manager
P - 9000 Funchal
Madeira
Portugal

Dear Mr. Margeridon,

Thank you for your letter to me dated November 27. I apologize for any
confusion which my letter may have caused; sometimes I forget that not
everyone knows what a bush pig is.

Yolanda and Boris, my two bush pigs, have been travelling with me for years.
Sadly, their brother Edgar died in the sauna at the Manadarin five years ago.
As bush pigs go, they're actually rather small: three feet long and around
200 lbs., although Yolanda has a tendency to gain weight if I don't keep an
eye on her asparagus intake.

May I assure you that my hogs are very well-behaved. In fact, I'm afraid that
all three of them have been spoiled rotten by attentive hotel staffs all over
the world. Usually they stay in their room listening to the radio, but on a
hot afternoon, they do like a dip in the pool. Most other hotel guests don't
mind much.

In fact most people find them lots of fun. Three or four years ago, the
pastry chef at the Oberoi told me that Boris had finished off the entire
dessert buffet in less than two minutes, while all the other guests clapped
and cheered him on.

We would all love to come stay with you and look forward to your
confirmation.

Yours sincerely,

James Wade

Mr. James C. Wade III
Case Postale 103
Montchoisi
1000 LAUSANNE 19
Switzerland

13th December, 1989

Dear Mr. Wade,

Many thanks for your letter of 6th December and information about the bush pigs.

We do sincerely regret, but we can not submit you an offer as only small dogs are accepted at Reid's.

We are so sorry not being able to comply with your wish and remain with kind regards,

Yours sincerely
REID'S HOTEL

D.A. Margeridon
Deputy General Manager

DM/MGTS

ISLAND HOTEL (MADEIRA) LTD.
Registered Office: Beckett House, 1 Lambeth Palace Road, London SE1 7EU
Company N.° England 328212, N.° Ind. P. Colectiva 500878897

4

JAMES C. WADE III

Case postale 103
Montchoisi
CH - 1000 Lausanne 19
Switzerland

November 18, 1989

University of Kentucky
School of Medicine
Attn: Bodies Committee
Lexington, Kentucky 40506
USA

Dear Sirs,

I would like to leave my body to science after I die. Maybe your
students could make good use of it in their research work.

Unfortunately most of my major organs are spoken for, but I could leave
you my connective tissue and one dozen lymph nodes if you are
interested. Could you please let me know how I should proceed with the
arrangements?

Thank you in advance.

Yours sincerely,

James Wade

UNIVERSITY OF KENTUCKY

Chandler Medical Center

College of Medicine

Department of Anatomy and Neurobiology
MN224 Medical Center
Lexington, KY 40536-0084
(606) 233-5155

December 22, 1989

Mr. James C. Wade, III
Case postale 103
Montchoisi
CH - 1000 Lausanne 19
SWITZERLAND

Dear Mr. Wade:

We are in receipt of your letter of 18 November 1989 advising that you are interested in bequeathing your body (your organs have already been donated). As our program is bequeathal of the entire body, an unconditional bequeathal, we are unable to accept you into our program. Also, our program is for residents of Kentucky.

We do appreciate your interest, but, unfortunately, are unable to accept you into our program.

Sincerely,

Gary W. Ginn
Director
Body Bequeathal Program

GWG:dm

An Equal Opportunity University

JAMES C. WADE III

Case postale 103 Montchoisi
1000 Lausanne 19
Switzerland

November 25, 1989

Lufthansa
Attn: Customer Service Department
Von-Gablenz-Strasse 2-6
5000 Köln 21
Federal Republic of Germany

Dear Sirs,

Recently I flew on a Lufthansa flight from Frankfurt to New York. While
en route I was very surprised that one of the flight attendants, a
blonde woman about 30 years old, removed one of the seats with a
screwdriver and gave it to one of the passengers as a souvenir.

I am sure this sort of thing must be against your rules. Clearly this
would have disastrous consequences for passenger comfort if carried to
its extreme. Will you please discipline this woman, and reassure me
that you do not condone this kind of "customer service"?

Thank you for taking this off my mind.

Yours sincerely,

[signature]

Lufthansa

Lufthansa Lignes Aériennes Allemandes
1–3, Rue de Chantepoulet, CH-1211 Genève 1

Membre de IATA

Mr. James C. Wade III
Case Postale 103
Montchoisi
1000 Lausanne 19

Direction commerciale Suisse romande
Tél. (022) 7 31 01 35
Agence et Réservation
Tél. (022) 7 31 95 50
Télex 22 508
Téléfax (022) 7 38 96 55
Case postale 501, CH-1211 Genève 1
Fret
Tél. (022) 7 98 80 50
Télex 415 522, Téléfax (022) 7 98 17 11
Case postale 1058, CH-1215 Genève 15
Escale
Tél. (022) 7 98 23 50, Télex 415 523
Case postale 177, CH-1215 Genève 15
Banque: Société de Banque Suisse, Genève
Compte No. C4-709.580.0

V. réf.	V. lettre du	N. réf.	Date
		BA/su	13 decembre 1989

Mr. Wade,

Your letter sent to our customer Service Department has been
forwarded to us for further handling.

In order to investigate this incident we would like to know
which flight you took. Please let us know the flightnumber
and date of your journey.
We thank you for taking the time to write to us.

Yours sincerely

Lufthansa German Airlines
District sales Geneva

U. Baldus
Manager - Reservations
and Passenger Sales Services

Siège Social: Deutsche Lufthansa Aktiengesellschaft, Köln. Enregistrement: Amtsgericht Köln, HR B 2168.
Président du Conseil d'Administration: Gerd Lausen.
Membres du Comité Exécutif: Heinz Ruhnau (Président), Dipl.-Ing. Reinhardt Abraham (Vice-Président),
Dipl.-Ing. Frank Beckmann, Dr. phil. Heiko Lange, Commandant Martin Gaebel, Dr. Klaus G. Schiede, Dipl.-Ing. Jürgen Weber (Vice-Président adjoint).
Form 4064 T-89 (CGN RH 2) 138/4 Printed in Germany

JAMES C. WADE III

Case postale 103
Montchoisi
1000 Lausanne 19
Switzerland

December 18, 1989

Lufthansa
Attn: Mr. U. Baldus,
Manager, Reservations and Passenger Sales Services
1 - 3, Rue de Chantepoulet
1211 Geneva 1
Switzerland

Dear Mr. Baldus,

Thanks for your letter of December 13. I do hope we'll be able to get
to the bottom of this incident, because I normally enjoy Lufthansa
flights so much, especially the view out the window.

I wish I could remember the exact flight details for you. I believe it
was in 1983 or 4. I was sitting on the left side of the plane, about 10
rows back from the men's room, but the rest is kind of hazy. I do
recall that the hostess in question was wearing a green sombrero, which
struck me as unusual for a German. As I recall, she also had enormous
biceps.

I hope this information helps you. I think too highly of Lufthansa to
allow one of your employees to dismantle your property and give it away
bit by bit.

Yours sincerely,

[signature]

9

Lufthansa

Lufthansa Lignes Aériennes Allemandes
1–3, Rue de Chantepoulet, CH-1211 Genève 1

Membre de IATA

Mr. James C. WADE III
Case postale 103
Montchoisi
1000 LAUSANNE 19

Direction commerciale Suisse romande
Tél. (022) 7 31 01 35
Agence et Réservation
Tél. (022) 7 31 95 50
Télex 22 508
Téléfax (022) 7 38 96 55
Case postale 501, CH-1211 Genève 1
Fret
Tél. (022) 7 98 80 50
Télex 415 522, Téléfax (022) 7 98 17 11
Case postale 1058, CH-1215 Genève 15
Escale
Tél. (022) 7 98 23 50, Télex 415 523
Case postale 177, CH-1215 Genève 15
Banque: Société de Banque Suisse, Genève
Compte No. C4-709.580.0

| V. réf. | V. lettre du | N. réf. | ha | Date | January 23, 1990 |

Dear Mr. Wade,

Thank you for your letter dated December 18, 1989.

We are very sorry about the unfavourable impression you had
as to the somewhat strange behaviour of our flight attendants
of that particular flight.

We have informed the offices concerned in order to take the
necessary steps for avoiding similar incidents in the future.
You may be assured of their full attention.

Hoping to have the opportunity to welcome you again soon on
board of one of our flights, we remain,

Sincerely yours,
Lufthansa German Airlines
District Sales Geneva

U. Baldus
Manager - Reservations
and Passenger Sales Services

Siège Social: Deutsche Lufthansa Aktiengesellschaft, Köln. Enregistrement: Amtsgericht Köln, HR B 2168.
Président du Conseil d'Administration: Gerd Lausen.
Membres du Comité Exécutif: Heinz Ruhnau (Président), Dipl.-Ing. Reinhardt Abraham (Vice-Président),
Dipl.-Ing. Frank Beckmann, Dr. phil. Heiko Lange, Commandant Martin Gaebel, Dr. Klaus G. Schlede, Dipl.-Ing. Jürgen Weber (Vice-Président adjoint).
Form 4064 T-89 (CGN RH 2) 138/4 Printed in Germany

JAMES C. WADE III

Case postale 103
Montchoisi,
1000 Lausanne 19
Switzerland

December 18, 1989

The National Museum of Science and Industry
Attn: The Medical Curator
Exhibition Road
London SW7 2DD
England

Dear Sir,

My grandfather was an amateur dermatologist who during his lifetime
travelled extensively all around the world. In his will, he bequeathed
to me his collection of 900 mosquito bites, and I wondered if you would
be interested in displaying them?

I look forward to hearing from you soon and wish you a merry Christmas
in the meantime.

Yours sincerely,

Mr James C Wade III
Case Postale 103
Montchoisi
1000 Lausanne 19
Switzerland

Date	**3 January. 1990**
Our ref	
Your ref	
Telephone	**01-938 8065**

Dear Mr Wade

Thank you for your letter about your Grandfather's bequest of 900 mosquito bites. I am afraid I cannot make any decision about this collection until I have a little more information. Are you speaking of samples of skin or are they samples of mosquito mouth parts? In any case, I have to tell you that we would not be able to promise to display the collection although we may be interested in acquiring it to form part of the national collections at the Science Museum.

I look forward to hearing from you and wish you a very happy New Year.

Yours sincerely

Jane Bywaters
Collections Management Division

Science Museum London SW7 2DD Telephone 01-938 8000 Fax 01-938 8118 Telex 21200 SCMLIB G

The National Museum of Science & Industry
Science Museum *London*   National Railway Museum *York*   National Museum of Photography Film & Television *Bradford*
Concorde Yeovilton *Somerset*   Science Museum Wroughton *Swindon*

JAMES C. WADE III

P.O. Box 103
Montchoisi
1000 Lausanne 19
Switzerland

January 17, 1990

The Science Museum
Attn: Miss Jane Bywaters
Collections Management Division
Exhibition Road
London SW7 2DD
England

Dear Miss Bywaters,

Thank you very much for your letter of the 3rd. To clarify matters, my
grandfather's collection consists of the mosquito bites themselves,
each mounted on an individual wooden plaque. If I'm not mistaken, there
are one or two chigger bites mixed in, too.

As my grandfather was evidently collecting data for one of his theories
of correlation, each plaque bears not only the name of the person
bitten, but also his or her height and weight, shoe size, and last book
read.

As you can imagine, I was quite excited to learn that you might be
interested in accepting this meager collection at the Science Museum.
After receiving your letter, I looked through these 900 mounted bites
in some detail to make sure they were in proper condition to send to
you. My grandfather was most active on this collection in the 1930s,
and I'm terribly afraid that on closer examination it appears that most
of the bites have healed in the meantime. Would they still be of
interest?

Hoping to hear from you again soon, I am

Yours sincerely,

James Wade

13

Science Museum

James C. Wade III
P.O. Box 103
<u>Montchoisi 1000 Lausanne 19</u>
Switzerland

Date	7 February 1990
Our ref	
Your ref	
Telephone	01-938 8065

Dear Mr Wade

Thankyou very much for your letter of 17 January clarifying the contents of
the proposed Mosquito Bite collection.

Now that you are able to tell me a little more about the collection I can
see that, unfortunately, it is not an appropriate acquisition for the
Science Museum. It is just possible that the Medical Sciences Museum at the
Wellcome Institute for the History of Medicine maybe interested in the
collection, and I will be sending your letters onto them. However, I cannot
guarantee in any way that they may be interested.

Thank you for thinking of us in this matter and I hope you will be able to
find a home for the collection.

Yours sincerely

Jane Bywaters
Collections Management Division

14

JAMES C. WADE III

P.O. Box 103
Montchoisi
1000 Lausanne 19
Switzerland

March 23, 1990

Mr. Peter Jennings
c/o ABC News
47 W. 66th Street
New York, New York   10023
USA

Dear Mr. Jennings,

Perhaps you have heard of the International Society for the Prevention
of Haiku Poetry. It is our belief that non-rhyming poems are inferior
to traditional, rhyming poems and that schools around the world should
stop teaching students that they can write any formless mass of words
and dignify it by saying it is poetry. We think this leads to
undisciplined minds, and that is bad.

In July 1991 we are holding our first convention in Altoona,
Pennsylvania to discuss the progress we have made around the world in
re-establishing the importance of rhyming poems in school curricula and
in introducing anti-haiku legislation in a few key countries (Japan
included).

We are looking for a strong keynote speaker for this important
gathering and wondered if you would consider doing us the honor of
addressing the convention on the connection between a society's
acceptance of free-form poetry and its rate of juvenile delinquency. Of
course our Librarian and Sergeant-at-Arms, Mr. Kargash O'Sullivan, will
be happy to assist you with any preparatory research.

As Chairman of the Convention Organizing Committee, I thank you for
considering this proposal and look forward to hearing from you soon.

Yours sincerely,

15

ABC News
47 West 66th Street   New York, New York 10023   Telephone 212 887-4040

Peter Jennings
Anchor and Senior Editor
WORLD NEWS TONIGHT

April 9, 1990

Dear Mr. Wade:


```
Why target Haiku?
Of all that needs opposing?
Why this spare, small verse?

Rymes do not poems make,
But grace and art and pure form,
Haiku can have these.

There is larger threat
In limiting of voices;
Making one-tone worlds.
```


Yours Sincerely,

Peter Jennings

James C. Wade III
P.O. Box 103
Montchoisi
1000 Lausanne 19
Switzerland

JAMES C. WADE III

P.O. Box 103
Montchoisi
1000 Lausanne 19
Switzerland

December 2, 1989

Edite Kroll
Literary Agency
12 Grayhurst Park
Portland, Maine 04102
USA

Dear Sirs,

I have written a number of children's stories which I think might be
good enough for publication. I would be very interested in submitting
them to you to be published, but I wondered if first, with your
experience and knowledge of the children's book market, you could tell
me whether I am on the right track with the titles I have chosen.

The stories I have written are entitled *The Evil Grown-Up, Fluffy the
Vicious Mastiff,* and *Kill those Cousins!* I'm also polishing up a
screenplay called *Robin's Big Car Accident.* I could imagine Jack
Nicholson in the cast somewhere.

I would love to be represented by you, and look forward to your reply
and advice.

Yours truly,

James Wade

Edite Kroll
·LITERARY·AGENCY·

12 Grayhurst Park, Portland, Maine 04102

207·773·4922
Fax 207·773·3936
Telex 294139 COMMA UR

January 7, 1989

Mr. James C. Wade III
P.O. Box 103
Montchoisi
1000 Lausanne 19
SWITZERLAND

Dear Mr. Wade:

Thank you for your recent inquiry regarding your
children's stories.

Unfortunately, I cannot even consider adding any
new clients to my very small list at this time and
so cannot ask to see your complete manuscript. I
would suggest, however, that in future letters to
agents, you provide somewhat more detail about
your stories than just the titles. It's difficult
to tell very much about your writing from the
little information you supply.

With best wishes for your work.

Sincerely,

Edite Kroll
(m)

Edite Kroll

EK/mby

JAMES C. WADE III

P.O. Box 103
Montchoisi
1000 Lausanne 19
Switzerland

February 15, 1990

Olay Company, Inc.
Attn: Product Manager, Oil of Olay
1 Far Mill Crossing
Shelton, Connecticut 06484
USA

Dear Sir,

Do you make a special Oil of Olay for dogs? My dachshund is getting
wrinkly.

If you do have such a formula, who stocks it here in Switzerland?

Yours sincerely,

19

Olay Company, Inc.
1 Far Mill Crossing
Shelton, CT 06484
Telephone: (203) 929-9092

Consumer Affairs Department

March 20, 1990

Mr. James C. Wade
PO Box 103, Montchoisi
1000 Lausanne 19
Switzerland,

Dear Mr. Wade:

Recently you contacted us about obtaining Oil of Olay for dogs. We
appreciate your interest. Unfortunately we don't yet make an Oil of Olay
product that's designed for the dermatology of a dachsund- or any other dog.

We enjoyed reading your letter and have passed your comments on to our
Marketing Department. It is nice to know that you are so loyal to our
products. This is one time it would be nice to say that Olay is going to the
dogs!

Thank you very much for writing to us. We like hearing from our consumers.
Please feel free to contact us at any time.

Cordially,

Paula M. Curtin

Paula M. Curtin
Consumer Communicator

00AQ73500010315

20

JAMES C. WADE III

Case postale 103
Montchoisi
1000 Lausanne 19
Switzerland

March 23, 1990

Institute for Oncology Problems
Academy of Sciences of the Ukrainian S.S.R.
Ul. Vasilkovskaya 45
Kiev, Ukraine
USSR

Dear Sirs,

I have an unusual medical problem which no one in Switzerland is able
to help me with. I found the name of your institute in a directory of
academic organizations, and I hope you can help me.

For the past three months my left foot has been making unusual coughing
noises. It is very disturbing, especially at night. All that hacking
keeps me awake.

Do you think it is possible that my foot has contracted lung cancer? I
used to be a heavy smoker, but I always used my mouth and lungs.
Anyway, I quit a few years ago.

It is vital that I solve this problem because professionally I need to
have two healthy feet. (I deliver aquarium gravel for a living.)

What could be wrong? I look forward very much to your reply.

Yours sincerely,

ІНСТИТУТ ПРОБЛЕМ ОНКОЛОГІЇ
АКАДЕМІЇ НАУК
УКРАЇНСЬКОЇ РАДЯНСЬКОЇ
СОЦІАЛІСТИЧНОЇ РЕСПУБЛІКИ

ИНСТИТУТ ПРОБЛЕМ ОНКОЛОГИИ
АКАДЕМИИ НАУК
УКРАИНСКОЙ СОВЕТСКОЙ
СОЦИАЛИСТИЧЕСКОЙ РЕСПУБЛИКИ

Institute for Oncology **Problems**
Academy of Sciences of the Ukrainian SSR

45, Vasilkovskaya Street
Kiev- 022
USSR
Tel.: 2667598
Cable: Kiev· Oncology

Fax 2639416

25, April 19 90

Dear sir,

I read attentively your letter from 23 of March.

Symptoms that you described do not testify to lung cancer.

However, if such a thought makes you anxious, I will recommend you
to examine carefully your lungs in oncologic clinic and when the
results will be negative, to see a therapeutist (the pains in foot
can be caused by metabolic disturbances), or an orthopedist.

I wish you a good health

Yours sincerely

Inga V. Kassianenko, Professor

ККДНК. Київ, Репіна, 4. Зам. 6-2638—1500

22

JAMES C. WADE III

P.O. Box 103
Montchoisi
1000 Lausanne 19
Switzerland

May 1, 1990

Hôtel Beau-Rivage
Quai Mont-Blanc 13
1201 Geneva
Switzerland

Dear Sirs,

A delegation of pygmies will be visiting Geneva shortly in preparation
of their setting up a permanent UN mission.

As their budget is limited, I have been asked to find out in advance of
their visit how many pygmies would be permitted to stay in one room at
your hotel. If they sleep crosswise, it is possible to fit up to four
in a single bed.

Would you please respond to me at the above address, giving as your
reference "PYGMIE"? Thank you very much for your help. I am looking
forward to receiving your reply.

Yours sincerely,

James Wade

Mr. James C. Wade III
P.O. Box 103
Montchoisi
1000 LAUSANNE 19

Our Ref.: SM/lr   May 8, 1990

Re: <u>Pygmie</u>

Dear Mr. Wade,

We acknowledge receipt of your letter dated May 1, 1990.

In response to your enquiry, we inform you that we can only accept one person per single room, or two per two-bedded room, regardless of the person's height.

Attached you will find a brochure and a price-list of Beau-Rivage. Should you need any additional information, please do not hesitate to contact us.

We thank you very much for your interest and look forward to hearing from you.

Yours sincerely,

HOTEL BEAU-RIVAGE, S.A. GENEVE

Mrs. Snuggi MAYER
General Manager

Encl.

JAMES C. WADE III

P.O. Box 103
Montchoisi
1000 Lausanne 19
Switzerland

November 20, 1989

Educational Testing Service,
European Office
P.O. Box 1109
NL – 6801 BC Arnhem
Netherlands

Attn: GMAT Administration

Dear Sirs,

As I am interested in getting on the gravy train by obtaining an MBA, I
would like to take your GMAT test at the earliest opportunity. Could
you please send me information on when and where the next test will be
given in Switzerland?

Also, is it allowed to bring a horse to the testing room? This would be
purely for personal reasons and would not be meant for cheating in any
way. My horse has a way of calming me down a lot, and I am sure my test
score would be higher if he could be with me.

I look forward to hearing from you soon.

Yours sincerely,

James Wade

JAMES C. WADE III

Case postale 103
Montchoisi
1000 Lausanne 19
Switzerland

January 6, 1990

Cito/GMAT
P.O. Box 1109
NL - 6801 BC Arnhem
Netherlands

Dear Sirs,

I have just received your brochure listing the next test dates and
places where the GMAT will be administered. Thank you for this
information.

As I mentioned in my original letter, for personal reasons I would like
to take the test with my horse in the room. He is quiet and I'm sure he
won't bother anyone too much. Would this be permitted?

I would very much appreciate hearing from you soon so I can put the
next test date on my schedule.

Many thanks.

Yours sincerely,

[signature]

EDUCATIONAL TESTING SERVICE PRINCETON, N.J. 08541

609-921-9000
CABLE-EDUCTESTSVC
FAX-609-734-5410

February 8, 1990

Mr. James C. Wade III
Case postale 103
Montchoisi
1000 Lausanne 19
Switzerland

Dear Mr. Wade:

CITO, our representative in the Netherlands, sent me
your January 6 letter which I assume was written in
jest.

You said you explained in your original letter to ETS
why you were requesting special testing arrangements for
GMAT. We never received this letter. Would you send me
a copy?

Sincerely yours,

Elizabeth Neilson

Elizabeth Neilson
Test Center Management

27

JAMES C. WADE III

P.O. Box 103
Montchoisi
1000 Lausanne 19
Switzerland

February 27, 1990

Educational Testing Service
Attn: Ms. Elizabeth Neilson
Test Center Management
Princeton, New Jersey 08541
USA

Dear Ms. Neilson,

As you requested, I am sending you a copy of my letter asking if I
might bring my horse along when I take the GMAT. I do not know why you
never received it. Maybe you guys need better management skills
yourselves.

Could you please give me your decision soon? I do not like tests any
more than Sugarfoot and am looking forward to having the whole ordeal
behind me as soon as possible.

Thanks in advance for taking the time to consider this special request.

Sincerely,

James Wade

EDUCATIONAL TESTING SERVICE PRINCETON, N.J. 08541

609-921-9000
CABLE-EDUCTESTSVC
FAX-609-734-5410

March 9, 1990

Mr. James C. Wade III
Case postale 103
Montchoisi
1000 Lausanne 19
Switzerland

Dear Mr. Wade:

Thank you for your February 27 letter enclosing a copy
of your earlier communication to ETS.

I am afraid you will have to sit for the GMAT alone.
Horses are not permitted in testing rooms.

Sincerely yours,

Elizabeth Neilson

Elizabeth Neilson
Test Center Management

29

JAMES C. WADE III

P.O. Box 103
Montchoisi
1000 Lausanne 19
Switzerland

June 29, 1990

Procter and Gamble
Attn: Product Naming Committee
Cincinnati, Ohio
USA

Dear Sirs,

Is it true that you have just launched a disposable diaper for old
people called GRAMPERS? I am 87 years old and find this offensive and
disrespectful. You ought to be ashamed of yourselves.

I hope that you will come up with some other name for these diapers,
and SOON!

On behalf of old people everywhere,

Sincerely yours,

[signature]

30

PROCTER & GAMBLE AG

1, rue du Pré-de-la-Bichette (Angle avenue Giuseppe-Motta) 1211 Genève 2, Switzerland
Fax: (022) 734 47 76   Telex: 22 378 PGGE   Central Exchange (022) 730 31 11

Direct line: (022)

Mr. James C. Wade III
P.O. Box 103
Montchoisi
1000 Lausanne 19
Switzerland

August 9th, 1990

Dear Mr. Wade:

Your letter of June 29 about GRAMPERS has been referred to us. We assume
that you saw this product in Switzerland where you have your address. Our
office in Geneva is responsible for the Procter & Gamble business in this
market.

We wish to advise you that Procter & Gamble does not sell nor make any
incontinence protection product called GRAMPERS. We do sell a disposable
baby diapers called PAMPERS all over the world and nobody has objected to
that brand. I can only surmise that you are mistaken in identifying us as
the maker of the product GRAMPERS.

Sincerely,

R.D. Cruz

31

JAMES C. WADE III

P.O. Box 103
Montchoisi
1000 Lausanne 19
Switzerland

July 28, 1990

Rolex SA
Attn: Customer Service Department
Rue François-Dussaud 3
1227 Acacias
Geneva
Switzerland

Dear Sirs,

My wristwatch, a 1944 Triple Z Timetronic MinuteMaster, has been in
perfect working order since I got it 46 years ago as a gift for my
graduation from the US Army's K-9 Training School. Last week the left-
hand doodad fell off, however, and now, believe it or not, it tells the
time backward.

I am sure this watch was manufactured by Rolex, because at the top of
the face, just under the "XII", is the word "Malabunka" which I am told
was the code name for Rolex during the war.

I remember distinctly that it came with a lifetime guarantee, but
unfortunately my dog ate it around 1952. Should I send the watch to the
attention of your customer service department for free repair?

Thanks in advance for your trouble.

Yours sincerely,

[signature]

MONTRES ROLEX
SA
GENÈVE

CONSUMER SERVICE   CABLES: ROLEX GENÈVE   1211 GENÈVE 24

DIVISION   TÉLEX: 427 070 ROL CH

Geneva, August 6th, 1990 RA/Lw

Mr. James C. Wade III
P.O.Box 103
Montchoisi
1000 Lausanne 19

Subject : 1 Non-ROLEX watch
          Our ref. A002031, your letter of 28/07/90

Dear Sir,

When reading your letter of July 28th, we felt like something
out of a spy novel and we are still puzzling about the question
why a peaceful Swiss watch manufacturer, operating in a neutral
country, should want a code name for its totally non-strategic
wrist watches during the war...?

We have attempted to look up the names Triple Timetronic,
Minute Master and Malabunka, all of which are totally
unfamiliar to us, in the usual registers but none of them are
known or listed. We have reason to believe that this is not a
Swiss watch but rather, one of U.S. manufacture ; however, we
admit that this is just a guess since we have frankly never
heard of any of those brands.

Therefore, in the unlikely case that you have a lifetime
guarantee for this watch (no such guarantee covers ours, by the
way), we are afraid you will have to find the manufacturer and
to convince him, if he is still around, that your watch should
be attended to at no charge. Unfortunately, we cannot help you
in this quest but we wish you the best of luck. And if you are
not successful, perhaps you would try a real Rolex this time ?

                              Sincerely yours,
                              MONTRES ROLEX S.A.
                         Consumer Service Division

                              Rolf Arnet

BOMBAY BRUXELLES BUENOS AIRES CARACAS COLOGNE GENÈVE HONG-KONG JOHANNESBURG LONDRES MADRID
MANILLE MELBOURNE MEXICO MILAN NEW YORK PARIS SAO PAULO SINGAPOUR TOKYO TORONTO

33

JAMES C. WADE III

P.O. Box 103
Montchoisi
1000 Lausanne 19
Switzerland

February 18, 1990

Continental General Insurance Co. AG
Attn: Property and Casualty Division
Seestrasse 356
8038 Zürich
Switzerland

Dear Sirs,

I have recently acquired a large buffalo carcass and would like to know
if your firm will insure it against decomposition.

I look forward to hearing from you and thank you in advance for your
reply.

Yours sincerely,

James Wade

JAMES C. WADE III

P.O. Box 103
Montchoisi
1000 Lausanne 19
Switzerland

March 19, 1990

Continental General Insurance Co. AG
Attn: Property and Casualty Division
Seestrasse 356
8038 Zürich
Switzerland

Dear Sirs,

One month ago I wrote to you enquiring whether it might be possible to
insure a buffalo cadaver which I own against damage through
decomposition.

Perhaps the reason I have not heard from you yet is because you need
additional details for the policy. I apologize for not furnishing the
following information with my earlier letter:

The item in question is a 3-year-old *Bison bonasus,* male, weighing
approximately 1600 lbs., dead, shaggy brown hair, blue eyes, and having
a commercial value of around $100 (US).

For reasons I am sure you can well imagine, it is imperative that this
matter be resolved pretty soon. Therefore I would appreciate hearing
from you as to whether your company is prepared to offer me such a
policy.

Thank you for taking the time to consider this request. I look forward
to your reply at the above address.

Yours sincerely,

[signature]

Continentale

Allgemeine Versicherungs-AG
Compagnie Générale d'Assurances SA
Compagnia Generale di Assicurazioni SA

8038 Zürich, Seestrasse 356
Postfach 1232

Telefon: 01-488 91 91
Telegramme: CONTIALLG Zürich
Telex: 817 656 CACL
Telefax: 01-482 35 80
Postcheckkonto 80-13 209-1

James C. **WADE** III
P.O. Box 103
Montchoisi

1000   LAUSANNE 19

Il Zeichen
Ul Zeichen   KB / am
Direktwahl Tel.
Datum   02.04.1990

Buffalo cadaver

Dear Sir,

We thank you for your letters of February and March 1990 concerning the insurance against damage through decomposition.

To our regret we have to let you know, that we are not in a position to make you an offer for such an insurance.

We apologize for not answering earlier and thank you in advance
for your comprehension.

Yours sincerely,

C O N T I N E N T A L E
General Insurance Company AG ·

JAMES C. WADE III

Case postale 103
Montchoisi
1000 Lausanne 19
Switzerland

November 22, 1989

Singapore Tourist Promotion Board
Bergstrasse 50
8032 Zürich
Switzerland

Dear Sirs,

Could you please tell me the name and height of Singapore's tallest
mountain? I am organizing an assault on the highest peak on each
continent, but Mt. Everest is too dangerous.

Many thanks for your assistance.

Yours sincerely,

[signature]

Fremdenverkehrsbüro von Singapur
Geschäftsstelle Schweiz · Bergstrasse 50 · 8032 Zürich · Telefon 01 252 53 65

MEMORANDUM

Date: 1st. Dec. 1989

To	James C. Wade III	From	STPB Zurich
Your ref:		Our ref:	**pb**

Subject **Your letter 22nd November 1989**

Dear Sir,

Thank you for your letter. It was not easy to find out the tallest mountain, sorry for the delay.

Bukit Timah Hill is the tallest "mountain" in Singapore with the high of 165 m.

Best Regards

Patricia Baj

38

JAMES C. WADE III

Case postale 103
Montchoisi
1000 Lausanne 19
Switzerland

December 6, 1989

Singapore Tourist Promotion Board
Attn: Ms. Patricia Baj
Bergstrasse 50
8032 Zürich
Switzerland

Dear Ms. Baj,

Many thanks for your reply to my letter. The very name Bukit Timah Hill
has inspired my assault team with awe and trepidation.

Could you possibly answer a few more questions about this mountain so
that we can plan our expedition in more detail?

a. Who, if anyone, has already conquered this peak, and when?

b. Assuming we establish base camp somewhere around the 50-meter level,
are there sufficient rest facilities nearby for my men? They
particularly enjoy roller skating and crossword puzzles.

c. Where is the best place to buy the following expedition gear in
Singapore: thermal parkas, glacier crampons, ice axes, cowboy hats,
honeydew melons, bowling balls, and Methodist songbooks?

Thank you in advance for all your help.

Yours sincerely,

Fremdenverkehrsbüro von Singapur Geschäftsstelle Schweiz

Bergstrasse 50 · 8032 Zürich · Telefon 01 252 53 65

James C. Wade III
Case postale 103
Montchoisi
1000 Lausanne 19

Zurich, 12th December 1989

Re: Your letter, 6th December 1989

Dear Mr. Wade

Please find the answers for your questions as follows:

A) Many Students have gone up to the peak of Bukit Timah Hill before and recently also, it's only a few hours climb (approx 3 hrs).

B) There will definitely be sufficient rest facilities for roller skating and crossword puzzles, afterall it's only 163 meters high.

C) The expedition gear which you have enquired are not in demand here. However, you can try getting them at the following store:
   ➤ Yaohan Orchard Departmental Store, 5th floor, Adventure Corner, Or-chad Road

Cowboy hats
   ➤ Yankee Traders Pte Ltd, 04 - 52 Shaw Centre, 1 Scotts Road, Singapore 0922, Tel: 7376201

Honeydew melons
   ➤ At any supermarket

Fremdenverkehrsbüro von Singapur Geschäftsstelle Schweiz

Bergstrasse 50 · 8032 Zürich · Telefon 01 252 53 65

Bowling Ball

➤ Equipe 101 Management Pte Ltd, 04 - 01 Kim Seng Plaza, 100 Kim Seng Road, Singapore 0923, Tel: 734 57 16

Methodist Songbooks

➤ Methodist Book Room Pte Ltd, 10 Mt Sophia, 131 - 01, Tel: 338 07 90

I hope, this will help you.

Best regards

Patricia Baj

JAMES C. WADE III

P.O. Box 103
Montchoisi
1000 Lausanne 19
Switzerland

December 12, 1989

The Honorable Edward M. Kennedy
United States Senate
Washington, DC 20510
USA

Dear Senator Kennedy,

Next August, the World Association of Mathematicians (WAM!) will be
holding its biennial conference to review some of the new binomial
equations. We do this every three years.

At the upcoming meeting, to be held either in Osaka or St. Louis, we
will have the special honor of presenting a new award to the high
school senior with the fastest recall of the quadratic formula. This
award will be called the "Oskar," named after the Father of the Square
Root, Bill "Oskar" den Hollander.

As chief organizer of this event, I would like to know if you could
honor us by speaking at this conference. Your keynote talk would relate
how mathematical experiences, for example using Avogadro's Number, has
helped you as a world leader.

We are more than willing to lend you any mathematical support you may
feel you would need for your speech. Mr. Fantomas Squigg, our research
assistant, would come to Washington and be completely at your disposal
for three weeks. Thank you for considering this proposal. I look
forward to your reply.

Yours sincerely,

James Wade

United States Senate

WASHINGTON, DC 20510

January 9, 1990

Mr. James C. Wade III
Montchoisi
1000 Lausanne
Switzerland

Dear Mr. Wade,

Thank you for your kind invitation to address the World Association of Mathematicians. I am honored that you have chosen me to speak at this event.

Unfortunately, due to a prior commitment, I cannot accept your offer. I regret that I am not able to give you a more favorable answer.

Thank you again for the invitation, and I wish you and those involved in the conference good luck for a successful and productive meeting. Your efforts are commendable and you have my best wishes.

Sincerely,

Edward M. Kennedy

JAMES C. WADE III

Case postale 103
Montchoisi
1000 Lausanne 19
Switzerland

December 12, 1989

University of Cambridge
Faculty of Astronomy
Cambridge CB2 1TN
England

Dear Sirs,

I have recently bought a telescope and begun to study the night sky.
Naturally I have also been spending a great deal of time with charts of
the constellations to learn the positions of the stars, planets, etc.

The map I have been using has caused some confusion among my friends
who also share this hobby. They say that the constellations on my map
are incorrect, even though when I compare the sky to the map,
everything seems OK. They say there are no such constellations as
"Emmanuel the Horse," "Kanko the Bone," or "The Big Carrot."

My map is dated 1924 and so far every star on it matches up with the
stars in the sky. I know it's an old map but could they have changed
the names since then?

I look forward to your reply.

Yours truly,

James Wade

UNIVERSITY OF CAMBRIDGE
INSTITUTE OF ASTRONOMY

The Observatories, Madingley Road, Cambridge CB3 0HA, England
Telephone: 0223-3375**22**   Telex: 817297 ASTRON G
Enquiries: 0223-337548   Telegrams: Observer Cambridge UK.

2 January 1990

Dear Mr Wade,

Thank you for your letter. We think you are having your leg pulled and should react accordingly.

Yours sincerely

M.F. Ingham
Secretary,
Institute of Astronomy

JAMES C. WADE III

P.O. Box 103
Montchoisi
1000 Lausanne 19
Switzerland

March 19, 1990

Collectors Service,
Swiss Postal Authority
Parkterasse 10
3030 Bern
Switzerland

Dear Sirs,

I understand that in 1921 you issued a 5-centime stamp in honor of the
400th anniversary of the invention of the Aztec typewriter.

My wife is a big fan of the Aztecs and I would like to surprise her for
her birthday with a couple of these stamps.

Do you have any left in stock? If so I would be willing to pay a 10%
premium over their face value.

Thank you for looking into this for me.

Sincerely yours,

[signature]

PTT

Schweizerische Post-, Telefon- und Telegrafenbetriebe
Entreprise des postes, téléphones et télégraphes suisses
Azienda svizzera delle poste, dei telefoni e dei telegrafi
Interpresa svizra da posta, telefon e telegraf

Generaldirektion	Direzione generale
Wertzeichenverkaufsstelle	Servizio filatelico
Direction générale	Direcziun generala
Service philatélique	Servetsch da filatelia

Hauptabteilung Wertzeichen
Wertzeichenverkaufsstelle
Parkterrasse 10
3030 Bern

✆ (031) 62 27 28
Telefax (031) 62 73 08

Telegrammadresse
Adresse télégraphique
Indirizzo telegrafico
Adressa telegrafica
Postphil

Postcheckkonto
Compte de chèques postaux
Conto corrente postale
Conto da schec postal
30-6456-0

Mr. James C. Wade III
P.O. Box 103
Montchoisi

1000 LAUSANNE 19

Ihr Zeichen	Ihre Nachricht vom	Unser Zeichen	Sachbearbeiter(in)	Datum
Votre référence	Votre communication du	Notre référence	Objet traité par	Date
Vostro riferimento	Vostra comunicazione del	Nostro riferimento	Oggetto trattato da	Data
Vossa referenza	Vossa communicaziun dal	Nossa referenza	Object tractà da	Data
19.3.90			1z	21.3.90

Dear Mr. Wade,

We are sorry to inform you that the stamp which you
wish to receive, a 5 centime stamp in honor of the
400th anniversary of the invention of the Aztec
typewriter, is not obtainable at our office.

We are sending you a list of stamp dealers where you
may enquire about the same.

With best regards, we remain,

Yours truly,

POSTAGE STAMP MAIN DIVISION
Philatelic Office

Gfeller

JAMES C. WADE III

P.O. Box 103
Montchoisi
1000 Lausanne 19
Switzerland

January 3, 1990

The Honorable Dirk Kempthorpe
Mayor of Boise, Idaho
City Hall
Boise, Idaho 83707
USA

Dear Mayor Kempthorpe,

In the year 1790, the renowned German physicist Traugott Spodler first
described the principle of hot plasma migration from an area of high
concentration to an area of not-so-high concentration.

To commemorate the bicentennial of this great discovery, my colleagues
and I here at PlasmaGog GmbH have commissioned the sculptor Barlon
Fanley to immortalize Spodler with a statue depicting him at the moment
of his discovery. As you no doubt remember from your own high school
physics classes, Prof. Spodler came to his historical revelation in a
dream in which he was spearing a goat, and Mr. Fanley's statue will
reflect this whimsical fact.

We would like to know whether the town of Boise would be interested in
making a permanent display of this statue in a Place of Honor in the
town, to be unveiled to the public on September 12, 1990?

Would you please let me know as soon as possible so that Mr. Fanley's
public relations agent, Mr. Bors Laard, can get in touch with you
regarding the details?

On behalf of PlasmaGog GmbH, I remain,

Yours sincerely,

James Wade

BOISE
CITY OF TREES

OFFICE OF THE MAYOR

DIRK A. KEMPTHORNE
MAYOR

COUNCIL MEMBERS
MIKE WETHERELL   DON BRENNAN
COUNCIL PRESIDENT   H. BRENT COLES
SARA BAKER   GARY L. SMITH
COUNCIL PRO-TEM   JAY L. WEBB

May 1, 1990

James C. Wade III
P.O. Box 103
Montchoisi
1000 Lausanne 19
Switzerland

Dear Mr. Wade:

Thank you for your letter regarding the placing of a statue
commemorating the discovery of hot plasma migration.

This is the Centennial year of statehood in Idaho and one of our
centennial projects is the placing of sculpture and other works
of art throughout the city. Unfortunately, at this time we have
more artwork than locations and we would be unable to properly
display the statue.

I sincerely appreciate your offer and wish you much success as
you honor Dr. Spodler.

Sincerely,

Dirk Kempthorne
Mayor

49

JAMES C. WADE III

P.O. Box 103
Montchoisi
1000 Lausanne 19
Switzerland

July 6, 1990

The Manager
The Gentilhomme Restaurant
Hotel Le Richemond
Rue Adhémar-Fabri 8-10
1200 Geneva
Switzerland

Dear Sir,

As a restaurant manager you are certainly aware that whenever one of your
dinner guests bites into a juicy hunk of meat, he is taking a gargantuan
risk: the awful risk of choking on his food and meeting an unpleasant
death. A death not easily forgotten by your other customers.

I represent the Heimlich Squad, a group of five Americans professionally
trained in the famed Heimlich Maneuver, a well-known first aid measure
which can save the life of a person who is choking. The Heimlich Squad is
a non-profit foundation dedicated to assuring that restaurant-goers
worldwide finish their meals alive. Besides our annual celebrity roast,
the Squad's main activity is to be on call in a particular dining
establishment so that any need for immediate Heimlich action can be met in
seconds.

We would like to volunteer to cover your restaurant on *Tuesdays between
6:30 and 11:00 P.M.* All we need from you is a permanently reserved table
with good visibility over the entire dining area.

I would appreciate your contacting me at the above address to discuss a
convenient starting date for my team. If you prefer, we could simply begin
to patrol the Gentilhomme from the first Tuesday in September. Thanks in
advance for your reply.

Yours in Heimlich,

[signature]

OUR MOTTO: "THIS IS NO CHOKE"

JAMES C. WADE III

P.O. Box 103
Montchoisi
1000 Lausanne 19
Switzerland

July 31, 1990

The Manager
The Gentilhomme Restaurant
Hotel Le Richemond
Rue Adhémar-Fabri 8-10
1200 Geneva
Switzerland

Re: Heimlich Squad Coverage

Dear Sir,

You might recall that I wrote to you on July 6, 1990, suggesting that
the Heimlich Squad patrol your restaurant *each Tuesday evening between
6:30 and 11:00*. We have not yet heard from you and would appreciate a
brief confirmation that this particular time slot meets with your
approval.

We also need to agree on a starting date for the Squad. Might I
recommend the first Tuesday in September? This is the traditional
opening of Heimlich season, marking the anniversary of the date on
which we saved Dr. Murd Allbeck from a nasty demise at the hands of a
medaillon de porc at the Waldorf eleven years ago.

I look forward to your reply, at the above address.

Yours in Heimlich,

[signature]

OUR MOTTO: "THIS IS NO CHOKE"

1875

F&B/JP/ii   Geneva, August 15th, 1990

JAMES C. WADE III
P.O. Box 103
Montchoisi

1000 LAUSANNE 19

Dear Sir,

In reply to your letters of July 6th and 31st, 1990, we found very
interesting your organization of Heimlich Manoeuvre, who can save
life of person who can be chocked.

On this matter, we would like to meet you in order to discuss the
possibility of knowing better about your manoeuvre.
Would you please contact us by telephone to fixed a convenient date.

We thank you in advance for your call.

                                   Yours in Hotel Richemond

                                   Joseph Panarinfo
                                   Food and Beverage Manager

Le Richemond   Genève   Suisse

JARDIN BRUNSWICK - 1211 GENÈVE 1 - TÉL. (022) 731 14 00 - TÉLEX 412 560 - TÉLÉFAX (022) 731 67 09 - TÉLÉGR.: RICHOTEL
Famille Armleder fondatrice et propriétaire

52

JAMES C. WADE III

P.O. Box 103
Montchoisi
1000 Lausanne 19
Switzerland

September 5, 1990

Le Richemond
Attn: Mr. Joseph Panarinfo,
Food and Beverage Manager,
Jardin Brunswick
1211 Geneva 1
Switzerland

Re: The Heimlich Squad

Dear Mr. Panarinfo,

Thank you for your kind letter of August 15. I have been trying to call
you, but for some reason I keep getting connected to someone in
Düsseldorf named Werner von Blentz, who says he never heard of you. Are
you sure your phone number is printed correctly on your letterhead?

In any case, may I assure you of the vigor and professionalism with
which we go at our work. Since its inception in 1979, the Heimlich
Squad has achieved an enviable record of 18 wins, 3 losses, and 1 tie.

Please let me know as soon as possible whether the times I have
suggested previously would be convenient for you to have the Squad on
active duty in your restaurant. I would like to stress that we are
acting strictly out of our sense of duty; we do not ask for any
compensation in either money, food (salads or main courses), wine,
dessert, coffee, cognac, or cigars. Our reward is in knowing that we
may save the life of someone who has bitten off more than he can chew.

I eagerly await your reply, and the opportunity to serve you.

Hail Heimlich!

[signature]

OUR MOTTO (STILL): "THIS IS NO CHOKE"

JAMES C. WADE III

Case postale 103
Montchoisi
1000 Lausanne 19
Switzerland

November 30, 1989

Christie's
6, rue Paul Baudry
F - 75008 Paris
France

Dear Sirs,

As contemporary art is becoming increasingly valuable these days, I wondered whether you were ever in need of help in providing your clients with expert evaluation of the works of lesser-known contemporary artists such as Georges Blotz or Memford "Karachi" de Glique.

Blotz was a close family friend, and I feel sure that I know his sculptures as well as anyone else alive. I myself own three of his earliest works, including "Screaming Midget on a Pony."

As for de Glique, I have followed his work for nearly thirty years and could, I am confident, distinguish his blue from his red and green periods. I personally own "God's Big Tool No. 2," one of his finest pieces.

You may already have specialists on these two artists; if not I would be only too happy to lend a hand in any future expert evaluation. My services would be entirely free, as I am interested only in the art and not in any fee or other remuneration.

Looking forward to hearing from you, I am

Yours sincerely,

CHRISTIE'S

Fine Art Auctioneers since 1766

Christie's France S.A., 6. rue Paul Baudry, 75008 Paris Téléphone: 42 56 17 66 Fax: 42 56 26 01 Telex: 648562

Paris, le 6 décembre 1989

Monsieur James C. Wade III
Case postale 103
MONTCHOISI
1000 LAUSANNE 19

Dear Mr Wade,

Thank you for your letter dated 30 november 1989.

We took note that you are a specialist of Blotz and Glique.

We shall certainly consult you when we will have some pieces
by these artists for sale.

Thank you very much.

Best Regards.

Guillaume DUHAMEL.

JAMES C. WADE III

P.O. Box 103
Montchoisi
1000 Lausanne 19
Switzerland

February 18, 1990

PALEXPO
Palais des Expositions et des Congrés
Attn: Convention Scheduling Manager
1218 Grand Saconnex/Geneva
Switzerland

Dear Sirs,

I am writing to enquire whether your facilities could serve as the venue for a major conference in May 1998. We expect some 5000 participants.

I am President of the Save the Plankton Foundation, which is dedicated to informing people of the danger posed by whales to the plankton swarming in the oceans. Although in absolute terms, whales are outnumbered by plankton, they are still able to inflict considerable damage on these tiny peaceable creatures, for example by eating them.

For demonstration purposes at our conference, we would need to have the following special equipment:

- a glass tank large enough to hold 35 tons of normal plankton

- another tank which could hold 15 tons of special "fast breeding" plankton (together with spillover tanks as appropriate)

- 2,000,000 gallons of seawater

- 40,000 gallons of strawberry sherbet

- 3 powder blue Chevrolet Impalas

I would be interested in hearing from you on this matter as soon as possible.

Yours sincerely,

[signature]

JAMES C. WADE III

Case Postale 103
Montchoisi,
1000 Lausanne 19
Switzerland

April 6, 1990

PALEXPO
Palais des Expositions et des Congrés
Attn: Convention Scheduling Manager
1218 Grand-Saconnex/Geneva
Switzerland

Dear Sirs,

On February 18 of this year I wrote to you on behalf of the Save the
Plankton Foundation to enquire about the possibility of using your
facility for a major convention (5000 delegates) in May 1998.

As of today, I have received no answer and would like to know when you
might be able to give us a preliminary reply. My organization is hard
at work to allocate our multi-hundred-dollar budget for this event and
would like to begin nailing down some of the costs involved.

One further question: Are your air conditioning facilities 100% spore-
proof?

I look forward to hearing from you.

Sincerely yours,

James Wade

Orgexpo Palexpo

Fondation pour la promotion et l'organisation
d'expositions et de congrès - Genève

Téléphone: 022/798 11 11 (20 lignes)
Télex: 422 784 expo ch
Téléfax: 022/798 01 00

Case postale 112, CH-1218 Grand Saconnex, Genève, Suisse

Palexpo, April 12th, 1990

Mr. James C. Wade III
Montchoisi
1000 LAUSANNE 19

Dear Mr. Wade,

with reference to your letters dd February 18th and April 6th
we have been trying to reach you by phone in order to allow us to
know a bit more about the conference you are planning for May 1998,
but it was not possible to find your phone number.

We would appreciate if you could call the undersigned after the
easter vacation, i.e. week starting April 22nd.

Looking forward to hearing from you, we remain,

yours sincerely,

Gisela Keckeis
Promotion Manager

JAMES C. WADE III

P.O. Box 103
Montchoisi
1000 Lausanne 19
Switzerland

April 20, 1990

PALEXPO
Attn: Ms. Gisela Keckeis, Promotion Manager
Case postale 112
1218 Grand Saconnex/Geneva
Switzerland

Dear Ms. Keckeis,

Thank you for your letter of the 12th of this month. Please accept my
apologies for not being available by phone. The Foundation is as yet
unable to afford one, but if our worldwide fundraising sale of 'Mr.
Kelp' brand plankton biscuits goes ahead as planned, we should be able
to get one soon.

I am afraid that the steering committee of the Foundation has decided
to hold our 1998 global expo out-of-doors, rather than inside a
convention center. Our insurance agents have determined that there
would be too much risk to the delegates as well as to the facilities
themselves from hostile plankton clumping. We will therefore hold the
expo in completely natural surroundings in which the plankton will not
feel threatened or provoked in any way.

I hope that we may be able to stage a similar convention in Geneva
after we have a bit more experience. Thank you in the meantime for your
interest.

Sincerely yours,

[signature]

PS. When the 'Mr. Kelp' representative comes your way, I hope you will
buy a box of these tasty little biscuits!

JAMES C. WADE III

P.O. Box 103
Montchoisi
1000 Lausanne 19
Switzerland

April 17, 1990

Better Business Bureau
2055 Wooddale Blvd.
Baton Rouge, Louisiana 70806
USA

Dear Sirs,

I am an American citizen living in Switzerland. In spite of my foreign
address, I still receive a lot of mailings from American companies
advertising various products and services. Recently, however, I have
begun receiving disconcerting telephone solicitations from an
organization requesting me to donate a part of my brain to needy
children.

This group calls itself "Cerebellum Donors of America" and claims to be
based in Baton Rouge. They ask that I have my cerebellum removed,
refrigerated, and shipped via air freight to a warehouse in Moline,
Illinois, where they will arrange for its redistribution to a selected
cerebellumless child. Never any mention of reimbursing my costs, not to
mention tax deductibility.

After a discussion with my doctor, I was advised not to proceed with
such an operation, for health reasons. Yet even after I have explained
to the callers that I will not be able to participate in their program,
they continue to call me and try to persuade me to undergo this
operation, which is clearly not in my best interest.

I would like very much to get these people off my back and hope that I
can turn to you for help. Thank you in advance for looking into this
matter for me. I look forward to your reply.

Yours sincerely,

James Wade

BBB Better Business Bureau

of south central louisiana, inc.

May 8, 1990

Mr. James C. Wade III
P.O. Box 103
Montchoisi
1000 Lausanne 19
Switzerland

Dear Mr. Wade:

The Better Business Bureau has received your letter of 4/17/90 regarding an organization that calls itself "Cerebellum Donors of America".

We have no file information of this group and they are not even listed in the telephone directory. We contacted a Neurosurgeon in Baton Rouge to discuss this. He stated that this is a very unusual request. He had never heard of this procedure being done with a living person. Nor has he heard of such a transplant. It may be possible for a terminally ill patient to donate cerebellum for research only, not transplants.

We hope this information is helpful to you. We do thank you for contacting the Better Business Bureau regarding this matter.

Sincerely,

Tammy T. West
Complaints Mediator

JAMES C. WADE III

P.O. Box 103
Montchoisi
1000 Lausanne 19
Switzerland

June 29, 1990

Mr. Jean-Marc Chatelain
Dog Breeding Services
Rte. de Penau 131
1052 Le Mont-sur-Lausanne
Switzerland

Dear Mr. Chatelain,

Would it be possible for me to rent a dog for six months? I would
return it in good condition.

I look forward to your reply.

Yours sincerely,

62

JAMES C. WADE III

P.O. Box 103
Montchoisi
1000 Lausanne 19
Switzerland

January 12, 1990

The Explorers Club
46 East 70th Street
New York, New York 10021
USA

Gentlemen,

I have learned of the existence of your club from Father Squamus
Pindaar, the blind surveyor so active among the Patagonians. He
informed me that from time to time your members have mounted
expeditions to find the elusive Yeti in the Himalayas.

I too have been intrigued for years by this mysterious man/beast, and
have read nearly every publication offering some explanation as to his
existence and whereabouts.

As it turns out, to my complete surprise, the Yeti's son is at boarding
school with my son, and it may very well be possible to establish
contact with him through this channel. If you are interested, I could
speak to my son to try to arrange an introduction, perhaps at Dads'
Weekend, which I understand takes place in October.

I look forward to hearing from you in regard to this potentially
historic breakthrough.

Yours sincerely,

JAMES C. WADE III

Box 103
Montchoisi
1000 Lausanne 19
Switzerland

March 14, 1990

The Explorers Club
46 East 70th Street
New York, New York 10021
USA

Sirs,

Just after the New Year I wrote to you about a potentially historic
opportunity to come face to face with the Yeti. In fact, I believe the
chance presents itself not only to meet and shake hands with this
legendary creature, but perhaps even to have a couple of drinks with
him at a tailgater before a football game at our son's prep school in
New Hampshire.

As I mentioned, this would all be contingent on his attending Dads'
Weekend at the school this coming October. Obviously I cannot promise
anything. But through my son, who has in the meantime become quite good
friends with young Bob Yeti, Jr., I think it may be possible to arrange
a meeting. Please let me know if you would like me to try and set this
up.

I look forward to hearing from you soon.

Sincerely yours,

[signature]

JAMES C. WADE III

P.O. Box 103
Montchoisi
1000 Lausanne 19
Switzerland

June 29, 1990

The Explorers Club
46 East 70th Street
New York, New York 10021
USA

Dear Explorers,

Twice I have written to you offering a hand in putting together the
first face-to-face meeting with the Yeti, and twice my letters have
gone completely unanswered. I find it difficult, at best, to express my
surprise and disappointment at your unwillingness to face up to such an
historical opportunity when it practically falls into your lap.

According to Bob "Stinker" Yeti, Jr., his father--The Yeti him/itself--
is prepared to undertake the nineteen-hour trip from Kathmandu to the
United States of America to attend the school's homecoming football
game on Saturday, October 27, 1990. His attitude seems to be "Publicity
be damned!"

While in the USA, he apparently is willing to grant one, and only one,
interview. Otherwise, all he wants to do is to go to the football
weekend, visit with his son, stop in quickly at his podiatrist in New
York, and then head back to Nepal.

Please contact me so that we can nail down the arrangements!

Yours,

James Wade

JAMES C. WADE III

P. O. Box 103
Montchoisi
1000 Lausanne 19
Switzerland

November 21, 1989

Goodyear Tire and Rubber Co.
1144 E. Market Street
Akron, Ohio 44316-0001
USA

Dear Sirs,

I hear you plan to introduce a reversible tire which you just turn
inside out whenever you need a better tread for the snow.

I think this is a great idea and would like to know when they'll be
available here in Switzerland.

Looking forward to hearing from you, I am

Yours sincerely,

JAMES C. WADE III

Case postale 103
Montchoisi
1000 Lausanne 19
Switzerland

January 6, 1990

Goodyear Tire and Rubber Co.
1144 E. Market Street
Akron, Ohio 44316-0001
USA

Dear Sirs,

On November 21 of last year I wrote to you enquiring about when your
reversible snow tires would be available here in Switzerland, but I
have not yet received your reply.

I still think this is a fantastic idea, especially for left-handed
people like myself. May I please trouble you to look into this matter
for me?

I would very much appreciate hearing from you soon.

Many thanks.

Yours sincerely,

[signature]

JAMES C. WADE III

Case postale 103
Montchoisi
1000 Lausanne 19
Switzerland

April 23, 1990

Goodyear Tire and Rubber Co.
1144 E. Market Street
Akron, Ohio 44316-0001
USA

Dear Sirs,

Last November 21 and again on January 6, I wrote to you about your reversible snow tires, but for some reason no one at Goodyear seems interested in answering my letters.

Nevertheless, such a product is so needed, especially here in Switzerland, that I have submitted it (what little I know about it, that is) to the International Selection Committee for the coveted Grunder D. Hemple Prize for Outstanding Achievements in Rubber.

Please let me know a bit more about it for the details of the award nomination. I need to know its total dry girth, molecular structure, and available colors.

Thank you for taking the trouble to send me this information, and good luck in the contest.

Yours sincerely,

GOODYEAR TECHNICAL CENTER ⊕ LUXEMBOURG

PATENT DEPARTMENT
L-7750 Colmar-Berg Luxembourg

Tel.: 8199-3648   Telex: 2523 GDYR LU   Fax: 8199-2662

Mr James C. WADE III
Case Postale 103
Montchoisi

CH-1000 LAUSANNE 19

Colmar-Berg, May 22, 1990

Dear Sir,

This is in response to your letter of April 23, 1990 addressed to The Goodyear Tire & Rubber Company in the United States.

Unfortunately, we were not able to trace your letters of November 21, 1989 and January 6, 1990 to which you refer, and we are a little bit puzzled by your reference to a "reversible snow tire" allegedly invented by Goodyear. We are not aware of any such products and would, of course, appreciate it if you would let us have more details about the invention you attribute to Goodyear.

In the hope that we can be of assistance to you, I remain,

Yours sincerely,

P Weyland
Manager Patent Department

ms

D3/JCW

69

JAMES C. WADE III

Case postale 103
Montchoisi
1000 Lausanne 19
Switzerland

June 5, 1990

Goodyear Technical Center
Attn: Mr. P. Weyland
Manager, Patent Dept.
L - 7750 Colmar-Berg
Luxembourg

Re: Your reversible snow tires

Dear Mr. Weyland,

Thank you so much for your letter of May 22. I am sorry that no one at
Goodyear is able to recall my first two letters. They were sent to
Ohio, a state known for losing things. Here are some copies for your
files.

Regarding the Grunder D. Hemple Award, I have recently had an
opportunity to speak to the chairman of the International Selection
Committee, Prof. B. Dornhelm Strothers, who advised me that my
nomination of your new tire was disqualified because of the lack of
supporting documentation. Apparently the award was presented instead to
a company in Egypt that manufactures rubber E-Z Grab slip jackets for
toast. You can read all about it in the July issue of *Bounce!--The
Rubber Weekly*.

I am sorry that things could not have worked out better for you. It
would still be nice to know when these tires will be available here,
though.

Sincerely,

James Wade

JAMES C. WADE III

P.O. Box 103
Montchoisi
1000 Lausanne 19
Switzerland

March 23, 1990

The Hon. Ugo Mifsud Bonnici
Minister of Education
Valetta
Malta

Dear Minister,

I would like to ask your help in fighting a terrible problem facing all of mankind.

I am talking about gland abuse. You may not realize it, but many people neglect their glands to such an astonishing extent that they must be removed, wrapped in tin foil, and discarded. Afterward, these people may suffer from a wide range of dysfunctional peculiarities, from the familiar "wimpy eyebrow" to the horribly disfiguring cerebro-intestinal stomach clot.

Last month I founded the Dormant Organization for New Glands (DONG) to help these people regain meaningful lives. Its mission is to provide them with replacement glands on either a permanent or weekly basis (depending on actual need and personal preference).

As the name implies, DONG is not yet active. First I need to find a good chairman who can take my message to the world. The chairman's initial task would be to address our international convention in Indianapolis in August 1992. His speech (together with slides where appropriate) must make an unforgettable impact on the thousands present.

Would you be willing to take on this vital role? Unfortunately I am not yet in a position to offer you an honorarium; however, it goes without saying that glands of every shape and size will be at your disposal (as well as your immediate family's) night and day. I certainly hope you will consider this request and look forward to hearing from you.

Yours sincerely,

James Wade

PS. I have asked Frank Sinatra to be the honorary vice-chairman and I think he is seriously considering it.

71

MINISTERU
TA' L-EDUKAZZJONI

MALTA

MINISTRY
OF EDUCATION

Il-Ministru   *The Minister*

ME/146/90

16th April, 1990

James C. Wade III Esq.
P.O. Box 103
Montchoisi
1000 Lausanne 19
Switzerland

Sir,

Thank you for your kind communication of the 23rd ultimo, inviting
me to address the first convention of the above mentioned Society,
due to meet in Indianapolis in August, 1992.

Much though I would have liked to attend, I regret to inform you
that heavy official commitments sheduled for that particular period,
would preclude me from doing so.

Whilst once again thanking you for your kind invitation, I take
the opportunity to wish your Committee every success.

Yours faithfully,

UGO MIFSUD BONNICI
Minister of Education

JAMES C. WADE III

Case postale 103
Montchoisi
1000 Lausanne 19
Switzerland

December 12, 1989

Harrods
Attn: Pet Supplies Dept.
Knightsbridge
London SW7
England

Dear Sirs,

I have been searching here in Switzerland high and low for an
artificial spleen for my dog. Do you have any in stock?

I would appreciate hearing from you at your earliest convenience.

Yours sincerely,

[signature]

JAMES C. WADE III

Case postale 103
Montchoisi
1000 Lausanne 19
Switzerland

April 23, 1990

Harrods
Attn: Pet Supplies Dept.
Knightsbridge
London SW7
England

Dear Sirs,

Last December I wrote asking if you sell artificial spleens. I have not yet received any reply and wonder if you might check to see if my letter was ever received.

My dog needs a new one very desperately as the old one, a Korean-made job with lots of metal screws and pins, seems to be falling apart, at least judging from the sounds my dog makes as he walks around.

I am unable to locate one here in any pet supply shop in the entire country. Can you please help me?

I look forward to hearing from you.

Yours sincerely,

James Wade

Harrods
KNIGHTSBRIDGE

HARRODS LIMITED, KNIGHTSBRIDGE, LONDON SW1X 7XL TELEPHONE 01-730 1234 · TELEX 24319 · FAX 01-581 0470 · REGISTERED IN LONDON NO 30209
TELEGRAPHIC ADDRESS — EVERYTHING LONDON SW1

1 May, 1990

Mr James C Wade 111
Case Postale 103
Mont-Cuoisi
1000 Lausanne 19
Switzerland

Dear Mr Wade

Thank you for your letter. I have only been here since February,
but, have no record of any previous letter.

With regards to your request for an artificial dog spleen, I have
made several enquiries and I am reliably told that such a device
does not exist.

Usually, if the spleen is damaged or disabled, it can be removed and
the dog can live quite happily without it.

I would suggest you consult a veterinary surgeon as soon as possible
to discuss the matter.

Good Luck

Yours sincerely

David W Barnes
Buyer
Pet Shop
sa

JAMES C. WADE III

Case postale 103
Montchoisi,
1000 Lausanne 19
Switzerland

November 18, 1989

Phoenix Bookfinders
P.O. Box 527
Plainview, New York 11803
USA

Dear Sirs,

Could you please help me find a copy of Pope John Paul II's latest
book, *God, Man, Dog and Bug: All Have Only Three Letters?*

Many thanks in advance for your trouble.

Yours,

James Wade

```
                    PHOENIX BOOKFINDERS
                     17 SHERIDAN COURT
                    PLAINVIEW, NY 11803
                      (516) 938-8192
```

March 2, 1990

DEAR MR. WADE:

        WE ARE STILL ACTIVELY SEARCHING FOR

                GOD, MAN, DOG, AND BUG

        THE TITLE HAS BEEN INCLUDED IN OUR WANT LIST OF MAILINGS TO
SELECTED DEALERS ALL OVER THE COUNTRY.   CURRENTLY A NEW CONCERTED
EFFORT IS BEING MADE TO FIND A DEALER WHO MAY HAVE A COPY.

        YOU CERTAINLY WILL BE CONTACTED AS SOON AS WE HAVE BEEN
SUCCESSFUL IN LOCATING A COPY.

                        SINCERELY YOURS,

                        PHOENIX BOOKFINDERS

                        Art Louis

JAMES C. WADE III

Case postale 103
Montchoisi
1000 Lausanne 19
Switzerland

November 21, 1989

Volkswagen AG
Postfach
3180 Wolfsburg 1
Federal Republic of Germany

Dear Sirs,

Have you ever considered introducing a car that runs on vegetables? It
seems to me that this idea could help solve the problem of our reliance
on oil, and would also be a great way to get rid of table scraps. Just
pour them into the gas tank!

Which vegetables do you imagine would get the best mileage? I have a
small garden with some spinach and tomatoes growing. Or do you think
more exotic veggies are better, like aubergines?

Thank you in advance for your reply.

Yours sincerely,

[signature]

VOLKSWAGEN

VOLKSWAGEN AG · Postfach · 3180 Wolfsburg 1

Mr. James C. Wade III
Case postale 103
Montchoisi
1000 Lausanne 19
Switzerland

Ihre Zeichen	Ihre Nachricht vom	Unsere Zeichen	Unser Hausapparat	Datum
		1780-drwei-te	2 21 90	12.12.1989

Dear Mr. Wade,

Thank you for your letter dated 21 November, 1989.

We work at vegetable oils which can be used in diesel engines. In Germany the most common vegetable oil is rapeseed oil.

Unfortunately we have no knowledge about vegetables as mentioned in your letter. We assume that the oil content of those vegetables is lower than in rapeseed.

Best regards,
i. V.

Dr. H. Heinrich

Vorsitzender des Aufsichtsrats: Dr. jur. Klaus Liesen

Vorstand: Dr. rer. pol. Carl H. Hahn, Vorsitzender Horst Münzner, Senator h. c., stellv. Vorsitzender

Claus Borgward Dr. jur. Peter Frerk Dr.-Ing. E.h. Günter Hartwich Dr. Martin Posth

Dr. rer. pol. Werner P. Schmidt Prof. Dr.-Ing. Ulrich Seiffert Dieter Ullsperger

VOLKSWAGEN Aktiengesellschaft Sitz: Wolfsburg Amtsgericht Wolfsburg HRB 215

Telefon (0 53 61) 90 oder bei Durchwahl 9 und Hausapparat Teletex 53619-0 = VWW Telex 9 586-0 vww d Telefax (0 53 61) 92 82 82

JAMES C. WADE III

Case postale 103
Montchoisi
1000 Lausanne 19
Switzerland

January 3, 1990

Volkswagen AG
Attn: Dr. H. Heinrich
Postfach
3180 Wolfsburg 1
Federal Republic of Germany

Dear Dr. Heinrich,

Thank you very much for your letter dated December 12, 1989. I will
definitely take your hint and plant some rapeseed this spring. In
fact, I think I'll plant the whole yard in rapeseed, if I can afford
the fertilizer and weedkiller and all that other farmer stuff. Could
you please tell me how many miles per bushel I should be getting?

Many thanks again for your reply.

Yours sincerely,

James Wade

VOLKSWAGEN

VOLKSWAGEN AG · Postfach · 3180 Wolfsburg 1

Mr. James C. Wade III
Case postale 103
Montchoisi

1000 Lausanne 19
Switzerland

Ihre Zeichen	Ihre Nachricht vom	Unsere Zeichen *uh'*	Unser Hausapparat	Datum
		1780-drwei-te	2 21 90	17.01.1990

Dear Mr. Wade,

Thank you for your letter dated 3 January 1990.

In Germany you can expect about 1000 l of rapeseed oil per
10 000 m² of acre.

If 1 bushel which equals concerning to our knowledge 76,2 kg is
processed to oil in an oil mill the yield is about 63,5 l of oil.

The mileage of the vehicle depends on the vehicle itself. Concerning to the lower heating value of rapeseed oil you can expect a
reduction in the mileage of about 10 per cent.

We currently are working on research projects on rapeseed oil which
are not ready for production.

We recommend at this phase of research not to invest own money in
such projects.

Best regards,
i. V.

Dr. H. Heinrich

Vorsitzender   Vorstand: Dr. jur. Peter Frerk   Dr. rer. pol. Werner P. Schmidt   VOLKSWAGEN   Telefon (0 53 61) 90
des Aufsichtsrats: Dr. rer. pol. Carl H. Hahn,   Daniel Goeudevert   Prof. Dr.-Ing. Ulrich Seiffert   Aktiengesellschaft   oder bei Durchwahl
Dr. jur. Klaus Liesen   Vorsitzender   Dr.-Ing. E.h. Günter Hartwich   Dieter Ullsperger   Sitz: Wolfsburg   9 und Hausapparat
                                                Dr. jur. Martin Posth   Amtsgericht Wolfsburg   Teletex 53619-0 – VWW
                                                                                                               HRB 215   Telex: 9 586-0 vvw d
                                                                                                                                       Telefax (0 53 61) 92 82 82

JAMES C. WADE III

P.O. Box 103
Montchoisi
1000 Lausanne 19
Switzerland

June 30, 1990

University Hospital of the Canton of Vaud
Rue du Bugnon 46
1011 Lausanne
Switzerland

Attn: Dept. of Plastic and Reconstructive Surgery

Dear Sirs,

I have a big, unsightly wart on my right hand. For personal reasons, I
would prefer to have it on my left hand, and I wondered if you could
tell me whether it is possible to have it transplanted at your
hospital.

You cannot imagine how pleased I would be if this could be arranged. I
look forward to hearing from you.

Yours sincerely,

JAMES C. WADE III

Case postale 103
Montchoisi
1000 Lausanne 19
Switzerland

January 9, 1990

Debrett's Peerage
73 Britannia Road
London SW6
England

Dear Sirs,

I wonder if you could help me find my ancestral roots. My parents are
unfortunately unable to provide me with much background information, as
the only family records we had were lost in a fire when I was quite
young.

I am particularly interested in tracing my mother's family tree. She is
a Sherpa. Will this complicate matters at all?

Yours sincerely,

James Wade

PS. I am not really in a position to pay you a fee, but if you have any
heavy objects you need moved, I would be happy to carry them for you.

Debrett's Peerage Limited

Founded 1769
73/77 BRITANNIA ROAD · PO BOX 357 · LONDON · SW6 2JY
TEL: 01-736 6524-6   TELEX: 8953130 ESPEPE G   FAX: 01-731 7768

Patrons: The Duke of Norfolk, KG, GCVO, CB, CBE, MC
The Duke of Richmond and Gordon
The Duke of Wellington, LVO, OBE, MC
The Duke of Abercorn
The Marquess of Bath, ED

Mr James C. Wade III
Case postale 103
Montchoisi
1000 Lausanne 19
Switzerland
                                                    16th January 1990

Dear Mr Wade,

    Thank you for your letter of 9th January.

    I regret that we do not have either the staff or the time to undertake
private genealogical research at this office. We would be able to give you
a limited amount of information if we were able to answer specific queries
from our own library, but, judging from your letter, I would guess that you
need a fair amount of basic research which would be beyond the scope of our
resources.

    There is an independent company, Debrett Ancestry Research, PO Box 7,
Alresford, Hants SO24 9EN, but they charge a fee for their services. I do
not know whether they require any heavy objects to be moved in lieu of
payment, but I rather suspect that this might not be a satisfactory quid pro
quo.

    If you do discover that your paternal ancestors were in any way connected
to the peerage or baronetage, I would be happy to help you; but otherwise I
regret there is nothing I can do.

                        Yours sincerely,

                        Charles Kidd

                        CHARLES KIDD
                        (editor)

*Directors: Ian McCorquodale (Chairman), R.M. Summers, FCA (Managing Director), D.M. Coughlan,
J.V. Porter, M.D. Preston, MA FCA. Company Secretary: N.W. Smith, FCA.
Registered Office: 86/88 Edgware Road, London W2 2YW.
Registered in England No. 1244105. VAT Registration No. 241 655 471.*

JAMES C. WADE III

Case postale 103
Montchoisi
1000 Lausanne 19
Switzerland

February 12, 1990

Debrett Ancestry Research
P.O. Box 7
Alresford
Hants SO24 9EN
England

Dear Sirs,

Mr. Charles Kidd of Debrett's Peerage in London suggested I contact you
about finding my maternal roots.

I am half Sherpa on my mother's side. She emigrated to America in 1947
to model Himalayan fashions in New York. I am not sure exactly where
she came from, but I believe it was at about the 14,000-foot level.
More than that I'm afraid I can't say.

Can you help me?

Yours sincerely,

[signature]

PS. As I explained to Mr. Kidd, I am unable to pay you a fee but
instead would be pleased to carry any heavy objects you need moved to
higher altitudes.

JAMES C. WADE III

Case postale 103
Montchoisi
1000 Lausanne 19
Switzerland

March 19, 1990

Debrett Ancestry Research
P.O. Box 7
Alresford
Hants SO24 9EN
England

Re: My Sherpa ancestry

Dear Sirs,

Thank you for sending me your very informative brochure on Ancestry
Services. Although you don't specifically mention any Sherpa know-how,
I am confident that you would do a first-rate job.

Regarding payment, I could certainly arrange to meet your requirement
of paying in advance, for example by carrying your burdensome loads
beginning immediately, or as convenient. I agree it is wise to set a
budget for the overall project, and would suggest that you consider a
total load of two tons to be moved 5000 feet higher in elevation
(broken up over several trips of course). You might also work this out
to be four tons moved 2500 feet higher, etc.

If you have any heavy objects to be moved here in Switzerland, I could
get started without further delay.

Please let me know if this form of payment meets with your approval,
and I shall see if I can get ahold of some basic information on my
mother's family. Unfortunately the only surviving document from the
fire that destroyed our family records is her 1938 Sherpa driver's
license.

I look forward to hearing from you.

Yours sincerely,

86

JAMES C. WADE III

P. O. Box 103
Montchoisi
1000 Lausanne 19
Switzerland

March 23, 1990

Danish Meteorological Institute
Lyngbyvej 100
2100 Copenhagen
Denmark

Dear Sirs,

I am compiling some information for a forthcoming book, to be called *A User's Guide to the Weather*. I am hopeful that you might be able to help me with the chapter on Scandinavia.

One sometimes hears of freak thunderbursts containing tadpoles, fish, etc., and I wonder whether you have ever recorded any of the following items raining from the sky:

- farm animals

- fresh vegetables

- canned vegetables

- caffeine-free soft drinks (if so, which brand?)

- Barry White albums

- primitive stone implements

Many thanks in advance for your cooperation, which I will certainly acknowledge in the book. I am looking forward to your reply.

Yours sincerely,

James Wade

Danmarks Meteorologiske Institut

DMI

F 0346

Mr. James C. Wade III,
P.O. Box 103,
Montchoisi,
<u>1000 Lausanne 19,</u>

9.054
28.3.1990.
DBA/Lis Juul
Lok.: 486.

Dear mr. Wade,

Referring to your letter of March 23rd, 1990 we regret to inform you
that we do not have any records of the items mentioned in your letter.

Sincerely Yours,

Stig Rosenørn,
afd. meteorolog.

Danmarks Meteorologiske Institut, Lyngbyvej 100, DK-2100 København Ø
Telefon 01 29 21 00, Telefax 01 27 10 80, Telex 27138 metobs, Giro 3 02 02 66

88

JAMES C. WADE III

P.O. Box 103
Montchoisi
1000 Lausanne 19
Switzerland

February 12, 1990

Calvert Social Venture Partners
Attn: Seed Capital Dept.
7201 Wisconsin Avenue
Bethesda, Maryland 20814
USA

Dear Sirs,

I have just succeeded in breeding a new and improved kind of dandelion.
To be sure, it still has the traditional ugly yellow flower, but this
new strain produces no seeds at all. So after one generation, this new
dandelion dies and leaves no heirs!

Two additional characteristics make my improved dandelions particularly
interesting. First, they greedily rob the soil of all the nutrients
that normal dandelions need. Second, after the normal dandelions
growing in the vicinity of the improved strain are thus weakened, the
"Wade dandelions" secrete a lethal juice which finishes them off. It is
a horrifying show of power.

My initial plan is to convince local governments to plant large patches
of "Wade dandelions" at strategic locations around the world, where it
will kill off the regular dandelions, and then, without seeds, die out
itself. Afterward, the world will be rid of dandelions forever.

I calculate that sales to government buyers will generate astronomical
amounts of cash! It will first require investment in a major breeding
facility and feed lot. I myself am willing to invest 4,000 dollars in
this project. I need another 9,000,000 to get it off the ground. Are
you interested?

Yours sincerely,

James Wade

CALVERT SOCIAL VENTURE PARTNERS, L.P.
7201 Wisconsin Avenue, Suite 310
Bethesda, Maryland 20814
(202) 659-0142
(301) 657-0866 FAX

April 4, 1990

Mr. James C. Wade III
P.O. Box 103
Montchoisi
1000 Lausanne 19
Switzerland

Dear Mr. Wade:

Thank you for writing to Calvert Social Venture Partners. We appreciate the ideas expressed; however, at this stage of our development we are not prepared to assist in the start-up of your endeavor. We agree that "to get off the ground" will be expensive.

Congratulations on your creative approach towards the traditional dandelion. We wish you every success.

Sincerely,

John May
Managing General Partner

Enclosure

90

JAMES C. WADE III

Case postale 103
Montchoisi
1000 Lausanne 19
Switzerland

January 10, 1990

Central Bureau for Statistics for the Netherlands
Princess Beatrix Laan 428
NL - 2273 XZ Voorburg
Netherlands

Dear Sirs,

I am compiling a statistical survey of the twelve member nations of the
European Communities, tentatively entitled *Lots o' Stats 'n' Things,*
and would be very grateful to you if you could provide me with the
following information from the Netherlands:

1. Annual squid consumption per capita.

2. Total man-hours slept by babies per day.

3. Average age of red brick buildings.

4. Length of road network, expressed in person-kilometers per cubic
   traffic.

5. Size of large rocks.

Thank you for your invaluable assistance.

Yours sincerely,

[signature]

centraal bureau voor de statistiek
netherlands central bureau of statistics

To: James C. Wade III
Case postale 103
Montchoisi
CH - 1000 Lausanne 19

your letter of:

our reference:
0960-DS-90

re: Voorburg, 25th January 1990

Dear Sir,

Your letter of 10th January posed the following problem for us.

Even if we were able to answer your rather strange questions, I am
afraid we do not have due time to pursue your practical joke.

Yours sincerely,

Johanna VIII

dir. sec.

voorburg, prinses beatrixlaan 428   heerlen, kloosterweg 1
                    p.o. box 959   p.o. box 4481
              2270 AZ voorburg   6401 CZ heerlen
         telephone: 070 - 3694341   telephone: 045 - 736666
               telex: 32692 cbs nl   telex: 56724 cbshr nl
cable address: statistiek voorburg   cable address: statistiek heerlen
               fax: 070 - 3877429   fax: 045 - 727440

JAMES C. WADE III

P.O. Box 103
Montchoisi
1000 Lausanne 19
Switzerland

January 14, 1990

Lakeshore Athletic Club
1320 W. Fullerton Ave.
Chicago, Illinois 60611
USA

Dear Sirs,

Later this year I will be moving back to Chicago after ten years away.
I would like to join a squash club immediately so that I could begin
playing as soon as I arrive back in town.

To help me decide which club would be the best one for me to join,
could you please send me an application form along with information on
your membership fees, facilities, etc.?

One important question I hope you won't mind answering is whether it is
possible in your club to use the squash courts for any other sports. My
local club here has been kind enough to allow me to practice driving
golf balls against the back wall. Of course I wear a helmet when I do
this. Would this be possible at your club, too?

Thank you for considering this request. I look forward to your reply.

Yours sincerely,

Lakeshore
ATHLETIC CLUB

Mr. James C Wade III
P. O. Box 103
Montchoisi
1000 Lausanne 19
Switzerland

April 26,1990

Dear Mr. Wade,

I have enclosed the package that we give to our new members.
It explains most of our policies. In response to your specific
question, we do not allow other activities to take place on the
squash courts.

If I can be of further assistance, please feel free to contact me.

Sincerely,

Walter A Reule
Club Manager

JAMES C. WADE III

Case postale 103
Montchoisi
1000 Lausanne 19
Switzerland

December 2, 1989

Hambros Bank Limited
Private Bankers
67 Pall Mall
London SW1Y 5EU
England

PRIVATE AND CONFIDENTIAL

Dear Sirs,

In 1984 I inherited the pelvis of a Sumatran rhinoceros *(Dicornis
sumatrensis)*. Early this year I mislaid it for almost six weeks and was
nearly ill with grief to imagine that I might have lost it.
Fortunately, it did turn up later, but I am quite afraid that one day I
really will lose it, and I have decided that I cannot afford to take
this risk.

I am sure that it would be best to keep this pelvis in a safe deposit
box. Do you have something suitable?

I look forward to hearing from you.

Yours sincerely,

95

HAMBROS BANK LIMITED

67 Pall Mall London SW1Y 5EU. Telephone: 01-930 1066
Fax: 01-930 8439 Telex: 883851 Attn. West End

James C. Wade III,   8th December 1989
Case Postale 103,
Montchoisi,
1000 Lausanne 19,   Our Ref: 5MJP72/CAB
Switzerland

Dear Mr Wade,

Thank you for your letter of 2nd December which I certainly found
intriguing. I quite understand your wish to use a safety deposit in the
circumstances.

Unfortunately, although a pelvis from a Sumatran rhinoceros would
certainly bring some colour to our vaults, I am afraid that I do not
think our facilities would be suitable.

Good luck with your enquiries.

Yours sincerely,

Michael J. Palfreman
Manager (Private Banking)

150 YEARS

Registered in England No 964058. Registered Office: 41 Tower Hill, London EC3N 4HA
Member of IMRO and TSA

JAMES C. WADE III

P.O. Box 103
Montchoisi
1000 Lausanne 19
Switzerland

April 23, 1990

Purdue University
Department of Agricultural Ailments
West Lafayette, Indiana 47907
USA

Dear Sirs,

Lately I have been feeling very run down and wondered what could be the
cause, since normally I'm full of energy. Then a couple of days ago I
noticed that my hands and feet seemed dry and discolored.

I can trace this tired feeling back to a dinner I had about two weeks
ago, where I am sure I ate some bad corn. Do you think I may have
blight?

I would sincerely appreciate hearing from you soon.

Yours sincerely,

James Wade

PURDUE UNIVERSITY

OFFICE OF THE DEAN

May 8, 1990

James C. Wade III
P.O. Box 103
Montchoisi
1000 Lausanne 19
Switzerland

Dear Mr. Wade:

Your letter of April 23 was passed on to me for an answer. We have checked with several experts in various departments within the University to get a meaningful answer.

Corn blight, the Department of Botany and Plant Pathology told us, is generally restricted to the leaves of the plant. Since we assume you did not eat the corn leaves we asked about other similar problems which infect the edible portion of corn. There is a fungus commonly known as "ear rot" which can cause respiratory problems if the spores are inhaled. However, they are thought to be nontoxic when injested orally.

If you experienced gastrointestinal problems, it would seem more likely that you may have encountered some form of food poisoning. Many bacteria cause this sort of problem without severe consequences. Food safety experts in our Department of Foods and Nutrition would be glad to address any further questions you may have about your specific experience.

We appreciate your confidence in Purdue and our ability to answer your questions. We hope our answers have helped you understand the problem you experienced. Please let us know if you have any further questions.

Sincerely,

Jon A. Story, Ph.D.
Professor and Associate Dean

JAS/jac
cc: Prof.April Mason

SCHOOL OF CONSUMER AND FAMILY SCIENCES • STONE HALL • WEST LAFAYETTE, IN 47907 • (317) 494-8210

JAMES C. WADE III

P.O. Box 103
Montchoisi
1000 Lausanne 19
Switzerland

July 27, 1990

U.S. Department of Agriculture
Attn: Director of Public Affairs
14th Street and Independence Ave. SW
Washington, DC 20250
USA

Dear Sirs,

I would like to find out more about your on-line database for
information on farm animals, OINKLINE.

Could you please send me a full-color brochure?

Thank you in advance.

Yours sincerely,

JAMES C. WADE III

P.O. Box 103
Montchoisi
1000 Lausanne 19
Switzerland

January 14, 1990

The Hotel Intercontinental
Chemin du Petit-Saconnex 9
1209 Geneva
Switzerland

Dear Sirs,

Would you be able to accommodate a group of 150 semi-professional
paranormal psychics? They are touring Europe along with their special
handlers and trainers to demonstrate their special telekinetic
abilities to various universities across the Continent.

There are some special requirements for a group like this. In the main,
such needs focus on finding ways to prevent members of the group from
communicating telepathically. It would be best if their rooms were
separated by lead sheets or slabs. If this is not possible, then we
need the radios in each room turned on at maximum volume during the
entire stay. This reduces their ability to concentrate.

To avoid temptations to levitate objects and cause embarrassment, the
kitchen should be outfitted with padlocks (especially on the
refrigerators). The rooms should have windows that cannot be opened.

Thank you in advance for considering these special conditions. I look
forward to your reply, addressed to me at the above address.

Sincerely yours,

James Wade

**HÔTEL
INTERCONTINENTAL
GENÈVE**

1211 Genève 19 · Suisse
Tél. 34 60 91 · Télex 23 130
Télégramme INHOTELCOR

**DEPT. VENTES ET PROMOTIONS
SALES DEPARTMENT**

Mr. James C. Wade III
P.O. Box 103
Montchoisi

1000 <u>Lausanne 19</u>

Geneva, January 18th, 1990

Dear Mr. Wade,

We acknowledge receipt of your letter dated January 14th and thank you
very much for your interest in Hotel Intercontinental Geneva.

Unfortunetely, we have to inform you that our property is not equiped to
host such a group and therefore cannot confirm your request.

We hope to be of greater help in the future, and in the meantime, remain,

Yours sincerely,

Marc Tassera
Director of Marketing and Sales

JAMES C. WADE III

Case postale 103
Montchoisi
1000 Lausanne 19
Switzerland

November 18, 1989

Jamaica Defense Force
Navy Headquarters
UP Park Camp,
Kingston 5
Jamaica

Dear Sirs,

From time to time you must have to get rid of old naval equipment that
is outdated or in less than top condition. I was wondering if you could
tell me whether you expect to have any destroyers or minelayers for
sale in the next few weeks. I would be very interested to purchase one
if I can get a loan from my bank. It would be fantastic for vacations,
even without any firepower.

Thank you in advance for your reply.

Yours sincerely,

[signature]

PS. I already have my motorboat license.

JAMES C. WADE III

Case postale 103
Montchoisi
1000 Lausanne 19
Switzerland

January 6, 1990

Jamaica Defense Force
Navy Headquarters
UP Park Camp,
Kingston 5
Jamaica

Dear Sirs,

On November 18 of last year I wrote to you enquiring about buying one
of your old naval ships, but as of today I have not yet received your
reply. Meanwhile I just renewed my motorboat license for 1990/91 and am
looking forward to another boating season. My bank has given me the
thumbs up for any amount up to $8,000 (US) on whatever seaworthy vessel
you might have for sale.

May I please trouble you to look into this matter for me? I would very
much appreciate hearing from you within the next few days.

Many thanks.

Yours sincerely,

James Wade

PS. How much do depth charges cost?

H.Q. JAMAICA DEFENCE FORCE
UP PARK CAMP
KINGSTON
JAMAICA

Kingston 68121 Ext 307

434

James C WADE III
Case Postale 103
Montchoisi
100 Lausanne 19
SWITZERLAND   *Ol* March, 1990

Dear Mr Wade,

     Receipt of your letters dated 18 November, 1989 and 12 February, 1990
are hereby acknowledged.

     Unfortunately, the JDF do not have any vessels for sale at this time
and probably not for the remainder of 1990.

     The delay in replying is regretted however, it is hoped that you will
find some suitable vessel in time for your boating season.

     With every good wish.

                                        Yours sincerely,

                                        J E PRESCOD
                                        Major
                                        for Chief of Staff

JAMES C. WADE III

Case postale 103
Montchoisi
1000 Lausanne 19
Switzerland

February 18, 1990

Jecklin & Co. Musikhaus
Attn: Records Dept.
Rämistrasse 42
8001 Zürich
Switzerland

Dear Sirs,

I would like to order a recording of Vivaldi's rare *Flatus Concerto No.
21,* but I have been unable to find a copy anywhere in the country. Can
you please help me?

Many thanks in advance.

Yours sincerely,

[signature]

Jecklin + Co. AG
Musikhaus
am Pfauen
Rämistrasse 30 + 42
8024 Zürich 1

Telefon 01- 47 35 20
Telefax 01- 252 45 03
Telex 817 728 musi ch

Sie erhalten

☐ *wie vereinbart*

☐ *zur direkten Erledigung*

☐ *zu Ihrer Orientierung*

☐ *zur Stellungnahme*

Mit freundlichen Grüssen
Jecklin Musikhaus

2.3.90/ta

Dear Mr. Wade,

Thank you for your order dated 18-2-90. We regret to have to tell you, that a Flute Concerto No. 21 by Vivaldi is not known to us. Perhaps you could give us further information (see enclosed photo copies).

Jecklin

JAMES C. WADE III

P.O. Box 103
Montchoisi
1000 Lausanne 19
Switzerland

March 9, 1990

Jecklin + Co. Records
Rämistrasse 30 + 42
8024 Zürich 1
Switzerland

Dear Sirs,

Thank you for your note to me of the 2nd and for the extensive lists of concertos for flutes. Actually, I was more concerned about Vivaldi's *flatus* music, which is something different. But no matter.

I was interested in using this unique melodic theme as background music on the soundtrack of a film I am making called *No Booze for the Dead,* which stars Rob Lowe as the young Albert Einstein. Perhaps you could help me find recordings of some of the sound effects I need for this movie:

1. Rustling of leaves in the wind (please no higher than force 3).

2. A small group of people reading technical magazines.

3. A Boeing 747 running out of gas and crashing into an erupting volcano (for a dream sequence).

4. Hundreds of Arab nomads attending a major-league baseball game.

5. A tennis match interrupted by the sound of three women exchanging small arms fire.

I realize that no. 4 may be a bit difficult for you to find here in Switzerland, but I sincerely hope you may be able to send me such a recording, on LP, CD, cassette, or 8-track tape. Thanks in advance.

Yours sincerely,

[signature]

JAMES C. WADE III

Case postale 103
Montchoisi,
1000 Lausanne 19
Switzerland

November 18, 1989

Ministry of the Environment
Myntagen 2
Oslo 1
Norway

Dear Sirs,

The Hill of Beans Club of Switzerland, a mountaineering and gourmet
cooking organization, would like to apply for your permission to re-
enact Hannibal's famous Alpine crossing in 1991 over the mountains of
Norway.

Our plan is to dress up as Carthaginian soldiers and march across the
Jotunheimen, accompanied of course by our 200 elephants, who would be
sent ahead to Oslo by Federal Express.

To help us prepare our trip we need some additional information:

1. Do our elephants need visas? Most of them have already had their
shots.

2. Once we have successfully crossed the Jotunheimen, can we all take a
comfortable, air-conditioned train back to the airport? If so, is there
a special supplement for the elephants in first class?

3. What is the local price of grass?

Thank you very much for providing us this information. I look forward
to hearing from you at the return address above.

Yours sincerely,.

[signature]

JAMES C. WADE III

Case postale 103
Montchoisi
1000 Lausanne 19
Switzerland

January 6, 1990

Ministry of the Environment
Myntagen 2,
Oslo 1
Norway

Dear Sirs,

Last November 18, I wrote to you enquiring whether you would grant
permission for a reenactment of Hannibal's march across the Alps over
the Jotunheimen, but I have not yet received your reply.

As it will take a bit of time to sew our Carthaginian costumes, train
our elephants to high Alpine conditions, and learn Norwegian, we would
be very happy to have the paperwork out of the way as quickly as
possible. May I please trouble you to look into this matter for me? I
would very much appreciate hearing from you within the next few days.

Many thanks.

Yours sincerely,

PS. It goes without saying that we will be bringing along our own
pooper scoopers.

MINISTRY OF ENVIRONMENT

OFFICE: MYNTGATA 2, OSLO. TELEPHONE NO. 47.2. 34 90 90
TELEX NO. 21480 env n – TELEFAX NO. 47.2. 349560
POSTAL ADDRESS: P.O. BOX 8013 DEP., N-0030 OSLO 1, NORWAY

James C.Wade III
Case Postale 103
Montchoisi   **6 FEB. 1990**
1000 Lausanne 19
Switzerland

                        90/214-2 NK OB/MBP
                        Ark 471.25

        MARCH ACROSS JOTUNHEIMEN

        Dear Mr Wade III,

        We have received your letters of November 18th, 1989
        and January 6th, 1990.

        You apply for our permission to march across
        Jotunheimen accompanied by your 30 elephants in
        order to re-enact Hannibal's famous Alpine crossing.
        You also have questions about visa requirements,
        transport and price of grass.

        We would inform you that in order to import animals
        to Norway, you have to apply for a permission from
        the Ministry of Agriculture.

        If your plan is to march through the National Park
        of Jotunheimen, you will need a permission from the
        management authority of the national park. The
        national park is managed by the County Governor in
        Oppland, the County Governor in Sogn & Fjordane and
        the Directorate for the Norwegian State Forests.
        It is quite uncertain if you will get a permission
        for your crossing, and the handling of an application
        will probably take some time.

        If you still prefere crossing through Jotunheimen
        National Park, you have to write a more detailed
        application, which contains information about your
        marching route, animals, equipment etc. The
        application is to be sent to the management authority
        of the national park.

As far as your other questions are concerned, our advise is that you contact the Norwegian State Railways about transport by train and the local farmers union about the price of grass.

We enclose some information about Jotunheimen National Park and a list of addresses and telephone numbers.

Yours sincerely

Kristi Vindedal e.f.

Ove Bakken

Encl.

JAMES C. WADE III

Case postale 103
Montchoisi
1000 Lausanne 19
Switzerland

January 3, 1990

Swiss Federal Intellectual Property Office
Attn: Phrase Theft Dept.
Einsteinstrasse 2
3003 Bern
Switzerland

Dear Sirs,

As an established author (*Eisenhower and Cauliflower,* 1981), I am concerned
that someone could ruthlessly exploit my talent by stealing some of the
careful wording which I have crafted over the years.

I am particularly worried about my metaphors, which won me a prize in 1983
and could easily be lifted, word for word, by some unscrupulous upstart
eager for fame at any price. My similes are good, too, but (so far) not
award-winning.

Is it possible for you to grant them special copyright protection? I
especially want to protect the following, which were cited as "classic
examples of the art" in Bardo McDillon's *Be an Author in 30 Days - or Just
Look Like One!*:

1. Springtime's ruby molasses dripped all over his aching brain.

2. After the last of Renfrew's head disappeared into the tar, we sat at the
   edge of the pit, harpooning the blowfish of sad and empty fate.

3. "Maybe you shouldn't hear this," I said. "You won't like it. Because, you
   see, you're nothing but a door handle, a bear trap, a fungus merchant.
   Yes, that's right. Even that." She sighed. . . .

Please let me know what steps I must undertake to guarantee that these
sentences enjoy the full protection of Swiss law. I thank you in advance for
your assistance and look forward to your reply.

Yours,

112

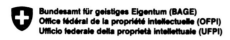

Bundesamt für geistiges Eigentum (BAGE)
Office fédéral de la propriété intellectuelle (OFPI)
Ufficio federale della proprietà intellettuale (UFPI)

3003 Bern
Einsteinstrasse 2
✆ 031 / 61 49 67

9 January 1990

Telex 912805 bage ch
Telefax 031 - 61 48 95
PC 30 - 4000 - 1

U. Zeichen
N. réf.
N. rif.   63/ST
✆ 031 / 61

I. Zeichen
V. réf.
V. rif.

I. Nachr. vom
V. lettre du   3.1.90
V. lettera del

Mr
James C. Wade III
Case postale 103
Montchoisi
1000 <u>Lausanne 19</u>

Dear Sir

<u>re</u>: Copyright, registration of

In Switzerland, as in all countries that are members of the Berne
Convention, literary and artistic works are protected automati-
cally once they are completed. Therefore copyright protection as
guaranteed by the Federal Law concerning Copyright in Literary and
Artistic Works does not need a previous registration or any other
formality. Our general information about copyright protection is
enclosed herewith.

We hope these explanations prove satisfactory and remain

Yours faithfully,

A. Stebler
Federal Intellectual
Property Office
Legal Service II

<u>Enc</u>: General Information (in French)

In einem Schreiben soll nur ein Gegenstand behandelt werden / Ne traiter qu'un seul objet par lettre / Pregasi trattare un solo oggetto per lettera

113

JAMES C. WADE III

P.O. Box 103
Montchoisi
1000 Lausanne 19
Switzerland

February 12, 1990

European School of Management
108 Boulevard Malesherbes
F - 75017 Paris
France

Re: Your MBA program

Dear Sirs,

I read your recent advertisement in the *Economist* and would be
interested in knowing a bit more about your program.

I am a graduate of Big Rapids Vocational Barber College in the United
States and now I would be interested in pursuing an MBA in order to get
the additional skills I need to make a go of my salon here in
Switzerland.

Can you tell me whether your MBA core curriculum includes any brush-up
courses on hair styling, clipping techniques, or wave management?

I look forward to hearing from you.

Yours sincerely,

James Wade

École Européenne des Affaires
European School of Management
Europäische Wirtschaftshochschule
Escuela Europea de Administración de Empresas

BERLIN
Europa-Center
1000 Berlin 30
TELEFON: (030) 25.48.02.0
TELEX: 184288 EAP D
TELEFAX: (030) 25.48.02.31

PARIS   OXFORD   BERLIN   MADRID

Herrn
James C. Wade III
P.O. Box 103
Montchoisi

CH-1000 Lausanne 19
Switzerland

4.4.90 JBP-st

Dear Sir,

Thank you very much for your interest in E.A.P. European School of
Management. Please find enclosed the latest publications of our
business school. I understand that you are interested in brushing-
up your qualification in the field of hair styling. Unfortunately
we don't have any special courses in this specific field of
management. As you will find in our program catalogue there are
not even any electives in the field you are interesting in.
Because I feel that hair management could be a very interesting
field of specialization in management studies I will put it to
the curriculum commitee of our school to deside whether we should
include an elective of this special sort.

I regret not to be in a position to give you any other
information. In case you have any further questions, please don't
hesitate to contact me.

Yours sincerly

Janine Berg-Peer
Recruitment and Promotion

CHAMBRE DE COMMERCE ET D'INDUSTRIE DE PARIS

115

JAMES C. WADE III

Case postale 103
Montchoisi
1000 Lausanne 19
Switzerland

November 25, 1989

Swiss Ski School
P.O. Box 351
3920 Zermatt
Switzerland

Dear Sirs,

I would like to give my grandmother some skiing lessons as a birthday
present this winter. She will be 93 years old. Can you please tell me
if it is possible to fix skis to a wheelchair, and if so, can you
recommend who I should contact to arrange private lessons for her?

Grandma's wheelchair is a SprintMaster IV deluxe racing model, 78
gauge, with chrome wire wheels, ABS and, of course, snow tires. What
kind of skis should I buy her which would work best with this
particular model?

Many thanks in advance for your reply.

Sincerely,

[signature]

116

Telefon 028 67 54 44 · Postfach 351 · CH-3920 Zermatt

Mr.
James C. Wade III
Case postale 103
Montchoisi

1000 **Lausanne** 19

Zermatt, 29 November 1989/TA/mr

<u>Your request</u>

Dear Mr. Wade

We refer to your letter dated November 25 and thank you for your interest in our ski school.

Concerning your question if it is possible to fix skis to a wheel-chair, we are sorry to inform you that we don't see a way to do so.

We regret not to be able to help you in this matter, but hope to welcome you to Zermatt some time.

Best regards
SKISCHOOL ZERMATT

Direction

Bankverbindung: Schweiz. Bankverein Zermatt, Konto 13.121.576.0

117

JAMES C. WADE III

P.O. Box 103
Montchoisi
1000 Lausanne 19
Switzerland

March 23, 1990

Burlington Industries, Inc.
Attn: Public Relations Manager
3330 W. Friendly Ave.
Greensboro, North Carolina 27410
USA

Dear Sir or Madam,

I am preparing material for a forthcoming book to be called *Universe of Socks*. I foresee a coffee-table type book which will be both a picture book showing socks from every culture as well as a historical overview of the development of socks.

As a leading manufacturer in the field, could you recommend to me a good sock journalist or other expert who could assist as an editor on this project? I am particularly looking for a knowledgeable man or woman who could write on "Socks at War" and "Socks in Industry and Commerce," the titles of two planned chapters.

Thank you very much for your help. I look forward to hearing from you soon.

Yours sincerely,

James Wade

JAMES C. WADE III

P.O. Box 103
Montchoisi
1000 Lausanne 19
Switzerland

June 24, 1990

Burlington Industries, Inc.
Attn: Public Relations Manager
3330 W. Friendly Ave.
Greensboro, North Carolina 27410
USA

Dear Sir or Madam,

On March 23 of this year I wrote to you asking for some help on a book
I am writing on our ever-surprising world of socks. At the time, the
working title for my book was *Universe of Socks,* but my publisher and I
have found a better name, *Lust for Feet.* I will be writing under my pen
name, Hullington Riga.

Almost three months have gone by without any word from you. I hope that
this is because you see the value of my project and have been spending
some time thinking about which sock journalists would be the best, most
reputable, etc. to collaborate with me.

I am being pressed by my publisher, however, and hope you understand if
I ask you, with a certain degree of urgency, whether your search has
turned up anyone who might be able to help me?

Thank you so much for your assistance. I hope to receive your answer
soon.

Yours sincerely,

119

JAMES C. WADE III

P.O. Box 103
Montchoisi
1000 Lausanne 19
Switzerland

June 22, 1990

Village Tourist Office
Attn: House/Apartment Rentals
7504 Pontresina
Switzerland

Dear Sirs,

In September of this year I would like to spend a vacation in
Pontresina and would like to know if you can help me find appropriate
accommodations for myself and my family.

We would ideally like to rent a big, rambling house, fully furnished,
somewhere a bit outside of the village, yet also far away from any
livestock.

I would also appreciate it if you could please inform me about any
special laws that may exist in the village regarding anthrax
experiments? I have been trying out a few strains on my daughter
(completely voluntarily), and I wouldn't want her to infect any of the
neighbors or their sheep.

Thank you in advance for your reply.

Yours sincerely,

[signature]

Pontresina 1800 m · Engadin

VERKEHRSVEREIN · TOURIST OFFICE · SYNDICAT D'INITIATIVE · ENTE TURISTICO

CH-7504 Pontresina · Telefon 082-6 64 88 · Telex 852 595 · Telefax 082-6 79 96

Monsieur
James C. Wade III
P.O. Box 103
Montchoisi

1000 Lausanne 19

Pontresina, 3th July 1990

Dear Mr Wade

Thank you very much for your letter. We'd really like
to help you looking for an accomodation in Pontresina.

We should know when are you coming to visit our village.
If we know the date, we can send you a list of available
flats ... even big, rambling flat where your daughter
will not infect the neighbors or their sleep!

You can simply phone us, in this case you'll have
soon our informations.

We look forward to welcoming you and your family
to Pontresina.

Yours sincerely,

Maura Romerio
TOURIST OFFICE
PONTRESINA

JAMES C. WADE III

P.O. Box 103
Montchoisi
1000 Lausanne 19
Switzerland

July 10, 1990

Village Tourist Office
Attn: Miss Maura Romerio
7504 Pontresina
Switzerland

Dear Miss Romerio,

Thank you for your nice letter of the 3rd. It is comforting to know
that you will do all you can to find an appropriate rental house for my
family.

I am afraid, Miss Romerio, that you might have misread my last letter
to you. Maxilla, my daughter, is a walking Petri dish, and as she is
chock full of anthrax germs at the moment, it really is the neighbors'
sheep I am concerned about, not their *sleep*.

If this would create any problems in Pontresina, you should let me
know. A few other towns in Switzerland have already forbidden us to get
anywhere within ten miles of them. Maybe Pontresina will be a little
friendlier?

Looking forward to your reply,

Yours sincerely,

[signature]

Pontresina 1800 m · Engadin

VERKEHRSVEREIN · TOURIST OFFICE · SYNDICAT D'INITIATIVE · ENTE TURISTICO

CH-7504 Pontresina · Telefon 082-6 64 88 · Telex 852 595 · Telefax 082-6 79 96

Mr.
James C. Wade III
P.O. Box 103
Montchoisi

1000 Lausanne 19

Pontresina, 20th July 1990

Dear Mr. Wade,

Thank you for your letter of the 10th and sorry for my misunderstanding.

I didn't really know what kind of illness "anthrax" was and I didn't want to tell you something wrong, so I asked more informations to our doctor. In Pontresina there are some sheeps (about 10 sheeps in the village, near the station and about 20 sheeps in Morteratsch, 7 km from here). Doctor Bezzola told me that if your daughter is treated (if she takes some medicenes) she shoudn't have any troubles and not even the sheeps.

I think you know better than me and Dr. Bezzola if it's the case to visit us or if that's too dangerous. From what I know, Pontresina has never forbidden to anybody to come here!

I hope you'll be able to visit our nice region.

Yours sincerely,

Maura Romerio
TOURIST OFFICE
PONTRESINA

JAMES C. WADE III

Case postale 103
Montchoisi
1000 Lausanne 19
Switzerland

December 2, 1989

The Natural History Museum
Attn: Plant Department
Cromwell Road
London SW7 5BD
England

Dear Sirs,

I have been reading a lot about the theory of evolution and even though
I have looked in many books, I still can't find the answer to an
important question I have. I was hoping maybe you could help me with
this.

Is it possible that a person could evolve directly from a plant? If so,
how long would it take, and would the person show any signs of having
once been a plant (strange complexion, roots, etc.)?

Thank you in advance for your reply.

Yours sincerely,

James Wade

**THE
NATURAL
HISTORY
MUSEUM**

Mr J C Wade III
Montchoisi
1000 Lausanne 19
Switzerland

Science Departments: Botany

Our ref   Your ref   Date   12 December 1989 Direct line

                                                                    Facsimile

Dear Mr Wade

Thank you for your letter of the 2 December.

I am not clear what you mean by 'evolve <u>directly</u> from a plant.' We are
certainly not aware of any evidence that would support this idea, except
to the extent that there may have been a common origin of life and that
plants and animals, as we know them today, may have diverged from that
source.   Modern classifications recognise groups of primitive
organisms that cannot be satisfactorily categorised as either plants or animals.

Yours sincerely

J F M Cannon
Keeper of Botany

The Natural History Museum Cromwell Road London SW7 5BD Telephone 0(7)1-938 9123
Statutory Name: British Museum (Natural History)

JAMES C. WADE III

Case postale 103
Montchoisi
1000 Lausanne 19
Switzerland

January 3, 1990

The Natural History Museum
Attn: Mr. J. F. M. Cannon
Keeper of Botany
Cromwell Road
London SW7 5BD
England

Dear Mr. Cannon,

Many thanks for your reply to my letter. You cannot know how relieved I
was to learn that there is no non-stop plant-human evolution.

However, this leaves me with the unsettling problem of finding some
other explanation for my neighbor's rather unusual appearance. I am
absolutely sure he contains chlorophyll. I wonder if perhaps he might
be one of the primitive organisms you mentioned which cannot be
categorized as either plants or animals. I will ask him and let you
know.

Thank you again for your letter.

Yours sincerely,

JAMES C. WADE III

Case postale 103
Montchoisi
1000 Lausanne 19
Switzerland

February 27, 1990

The Pet Registry
4748 N. Keystone Ave.
Chicago, Illinois
USA

Dear Sirs,

After a very long trail of dead ends, I have been referred to you by
Harvey Quackenbush at the Illinois State Department of Animals, who
said you have a neutered male spiny echidna for sale.

Could I trouble you to write me and let me know how much he costs as
well as how much you would charge for shipping him via air cargo to
Switzerland?

Thank you very much for your help.

Yours sincerely,

[signature]

JAMES C. WADE III

Case postale 103
Montchoisi
1000 Lausanne 19
Switzerland

May 1, 1990

The Pet Registry
4748 N. Keystone Ave.
Chicago, Illinois
USA

Dear Sirs,

About two months ago I wrote to you enquiring after your spiny echidna,
but my letter may have gone astray, as I have not received any reply to
date.

Since then I have spoken again to Mr. Quackenbush and he says he thinks
you have not yet sold him (the echidna, that is, not Mr. Quackenbush).
If this is the case, I would really appreciate your letting me know
what your sale conditions are and how much you would charge for
freight.

Also: Would you insure him in case he turns up dead?

Yours sincerely,

James Wade

PS. Don't forget the air holes.

May 23, 1990

Mr. James C. Wade III
Case Postale 103
Montchoisi
1000 Lausanne 19
Switzerland

Dear Mr. Wade:

I'm sorry for the delay in responding to your letters, but I fear you will
not be happy to learn you have reached another dead end.

When I received your first letter in March, frankly, I had to go to a
dictionary and find out what a spiny echidna was. Thinking I might
be able to help you in locating one, I called the Lincoln Park Zoo in
Chicago and asked them about the echidna. The lady I talked to said they
have had them at the zoo. When I read your letter to her over the phone,
her reaction was that, even if I could locate one for you, the chances of
it surviving the trip were not good.

Since the spiny echidna is indigenous to Australia, Tasmania and New
Guinea (I got that out of the dictionary) perhaps your best course of
action would be to contact the Export Development Offices in those
countries (but you probably did that already).

Sorry I could not be of any help to you, but I do wish you good luck in
your search.

                          Sincerely,

                          May Trapalis
                          May Trapalis

JAMES C. WADE III

P.O. Box 103
Montchoisi
1000 Lausanne 19
Switzerland

April 17, 1990

Mövenpick Corporation
Ice Cream Department
Zürichstrasse 106
8134 Adliswil/Zürich
Switzerland

Dear Sirs,

On a recent trip to the United States, I experienced a unique taste
treat which I thought you might be interested in hearing about. The
American ice cream chain Frostbite Charlie's has learned how to make
exquisite ice cream in many natural flavors I have never seen here in
Switzerland.

For example, I had a delicious cone consisting of one scoop of "fish
stick" and one scoop of "green bean" ice cream. My wife had a
combination of "roast beef" and "peas'n'carrots." She said the flavor
was very realistic.

Could the Americans be so far ahead of you in ice cream technology? I
certainly hope not. I look forward to your comments.

Yours sincerely,

[signature]

MÖVENPICK
PREMIUM PRODUCTS
INTERNATIONAL

James C. Wade III
P.O.Box 103
Montchoisi

1000 Lausanne 19

7. Mai 1990
HPD/ls

Dear Mr. Wade

I would like to thank you for your kind letter dated April 17, with respect of the latest experience you have made in the United States with new ice cream flavours.

I would like to confirm you that in the past we have produced new ice cream flavours, which go in the same direction as what you have seen in the U.S.A. However, these type of flavours can never become bestsellers immediately. At the same time I can invite you this month to the Mövenpick restaurants all over Switzerland where we serve as our monthly speciality a Lime ice cream with carrot pieces. We are continuously creating new flavours and ideas to test them in our own restaurant organisation.

With respect to the technology we believe that the europeans are ahead of the american technology. On the other hand it seems much easier in the United States to break through with the right marketing strategy than it is in Europe. In the meantime we have started manufacturing Mövenpick Swiss Premium Ice Cream in California and are selling it in three super market chains in Central and Northern California.

Considering the european gourmet sensation, which we can offer in all the Mövenpick hotels and restaurants around the world, we feel it rather discouraging how the quality of the frozen joghurt in United States is sold today without flavour intensity. The US have the highest ice cream consumption /capita with over 20 liters, where the swiss people have the highest joghurt consumption in the world, with 15 kilos.

Please find enclosed the Mövenpick Holding annual report to learn more about our activities.

Yours sincerely

i. A.

Hans Peter Dietrich
Technical Director

ZÜRICHSTRASSE 67
CH-8134 ADLISWIL
PHONE   0041/1/712 22 22
TELEFAX 0041/1/710 42 12
        0041/1/712 22 56
TELEX   826 744 MPZV-CH

THE ORIGINAL SWISS PREMIUM PRODUCTS

JAMES C. WADE III

P.O. Box 103
Montchoisi
1000 Lausanne 19
Switzerland

January 6, 1990

Hotel Bellevue Gstaad
Attn: The Manager
3780 Gstaad
Switzerland

Dear Sir,

Do you have a honeymoon suite? If so, I would be interested in
reserving it for two weeks next June.

In case you don't have an "officially" designated honeymoon suite, then
I would like a large, quiet room with an outstanding view, canopy bed
if available, ceiling fan, jacuzzi or private sauna, manacles and leg
irons, a selection of leather garments and accessories, with fresh
roses and champagne brought up daily, croissants, poached eggs on
toast, a side order of Canadian bacon, two coffees, one large orange
juice, extra butter and jam, and the *International Herald Tribune* all
on a silver tray.

I look forward to hearing from you.

Yours sincerely,

[signature]

☆ ☆ ☆ ☆
GRAND HOTEL

CH 3780 GSTAAD
TEL. 030 - 831 71
TELEX 92 22 32
Fax 030 - 4 21 36

Mr James C. Wade
Case postale 103
Montchoisi

1000 <u>LAUSANNE 19</u>

Gstaad, 28 January 1990 / jb

Dear Mr Wade

In reply to your letter of 6 January, we thank you kindly for your
enquiry about our "honeymoon suite".

Regrettably however, we are not in a position to accommodate your
rather special requests.

Your understanding in this matter is most appreciated.

Yours sincerely

Hotel Bellevue Gstaad
      Grand Hotel

p.p. *Buske*

Bodo Schöps
Director

Banques: Crédit Suisse, Gstaad: No de compte 00339–142540–51
Banque Cantonale de Berne, Gstaad: No de compte 401.501.6.16

133

JAMES C. WADE III

Case postale 103
Montchoisi
1000 Lausanne 19
Switzerland

November 22, 1989

The Ministry of Culture and Science
14 Aristidou Street
Athens, Greece

Dear Sirs,

I have read a great deal about the legendary Achilles, a man I admire
greatly. I would like to apply for your permission to mount a major
archaeological expedition to find and excavate his heel, which could be
displayed as a lesson to all of mankind.

Will you please grant me the necessary permits to begin digging
immediately? Thank you for your speedy reply.

Yours sincerely,

PS. Where do you think it is?

JAMES C. WADE III

Case postale 103 Montchoisi
1000 Lausanne 19
Switzerland

January 6, 1990

The Ministry of Culture and Science
14 Aristidou Street
Athens, Greece

Dear Sirs,

On November 22, 1989 I wrote to you inquiring about permission to
excavate Achilles' heel, but I have not yet received your reply. In the
meantime you'll be happy to know that I have purchased 20 bulldozers to
assist in the painstaking excavation work and am hiring 300 archaeology
students from the University of Alabama. Now all I need to know is when
the Achilles Expedition should be slotted into my schedule.

May I please trouble you to look into this matter for me? I would very
much appreciate hearing from you within the next few days.

Many thanks.

Yours sincerely,

James Wade

PS. Don't forget I still need to know where you think we should start
digging! Would down-town Athens be OK?

AMERICAN SCHOOL OF CLASSICAL STUDIES
54 SOUIDIAS STREET, 106 76 ATHENS
FAX: (301) 721 2208

ΑΜΕΡΙΚΑΝΙΚΗ ΣΧΟΛΗ ΚΛΑΣΙΚΩΝ ΣΠΟΥΔΩΝ
ΟΔΟΣ ΣΟΥΗΔΙΑΣ 54, 106 76 ΑΘΗΝΑΙ
ΤΗΛ. 723 6313

14 February 1990

Mr. James C. Wade III
Case postale 103
Montchoisi
1000 Lausanne 19
Switzerland

Dear Mr. Wade,

    The Greek Ministry of Culture has passed on to me your letters to them of November 22, 1989, and January 6, 1990, about your wish to excavate the heel of Achilles. Unfortunately, I must tell you that the heel probably no longer exists, if it ever did exist in the first place, since Achilles is a legendary figure with no historic personality. Since it does not exist, there is obviously no possibility of excavating it. Thank you, however, for your interest.

Sincerely yours,

William D.E. Coulson
Director

WDEC:nm
cc. Ministry of Culture

JAMES C. WADE III

P.O. Box 103
Montchoisi
1000 Lausanne 19
Switzerland

March 14, 1990

Cambio & Valorenbank
Attn: Mr. Cambio
Utoquai 55
8008 Zürich
Switzerland

Dear Mr. Cambio,

I am very interested in trading spaghetti futures. Thanks to my
background in agribusiness, I am sure I could make a heap of cash in
noodle options and other pasta instruments.

Could you please let me know the conditions for opening a commodities
trading account with yourselves?

Thank you in advance.

Yours sincerely,

**Cambio +
Valoren Bank**

Mr. James C. Wade III
P O Box 103
Montchoisi

1000 Lausanne 19

Zurich, March 19, 1990 BA/dp

Dear Mr. Wade

We refer to your letter of March 14, 1990 for which we thank you
vey much.

We have to inform you, that we do not trade in any commodity at
all.

Thanking you for having contacted us, we remain,

                              Very truly yours,

                              CAMBIO + VALOREN BANK

JAMES C. WADE III

P.O. Box 103
Montchoisi
1000 Lausanne 19
Switzerland

June 29, 1990

Adolph Coors Co.
Attn: Vice President of Brewing
BC 350
Golden, Colorado 80401
USA

Dear Sir,

I have been a great fan of your beer since before I was born. It is the
best there is.

An idea occurred to me recently and I thought it might be useful to
you:

Everybody knows that beer is brewed from hops. Furthermore, everybody
knows that when you drink beer, sometimes you like to have a few
peanuts or munchies to eat. Follow me so far?

Well, what about making a new kind of beer that is 100% brewed from
potato chips? It could taste like beer *and* Pringles at the same time!
As it is slaking your gigantic thirst it is also satisfying your urge
for munchies.

Would you be interested in developing this idea? I am not looking to
make any money out of it, just a free case once in a while. I look
forward to your reaction.

Yours sincerely,

[signature]

Coors

Coors Brewing Company
Golden, Colorado 80401

James C. Wade, III
P.O.Box 103
Montchoisi
1000 Lausanne 19
Switzerland

July 12, 1990

Dear Mr. Wade:

Thank you for your kind comments about our beer.   It's always
gratifying to know our efforts are appreciated!

Although it is certainly intriguing, we unfortunately will not be
able to develop your idea.   We wish you success in your future
endeavours.

Sincerely,

John Coors
Vice President, Brewing

JAMES C. WADE III

P.O. Box 103
Montchoisi
1000 Lausanne 19
Switzerland

July 14, 1990

Club Med
28, Quai Général-Guisan
1204 Geneva
Switzerland

Re: Summer vacation plan

Dear Sirs,

Do you have a good wrestling vacation? I am interested in spending a
few days in a quiet, very sunny place where I can meet nice people with
good tans and wrestle them.

I look forward to hearing from you soon.

Yours sincerely,

[signature]

Club Med

Geneva, 18th July 1990

Dear Sir,
We indeed do not have wrestling in our villages
but should you be interested in any of our resorts
abandoning for 1 or 2 weeks your favorite sport
please do not hesitate to contac me on 28 11 44.
Yours sincerely,

Béatrice GUERINEAU

CLUB MÉDITERRANÉE (SUISSE) SA
28, QUAI GÉNÉRAL-GUISAN · 1204 GENÈVE
TÉL. 022 / 28 11 44 · TÉLEX 421 229 · FAX 022 / 29 78 29

JAMES C. WADE III

Case postale 103
Montchoisi
1000 Lausanne 19
Switzerland

January 6, 1990

Habsburg Feldman SA Auctioneers
Rue Mont-Blanc 1
1201 Geneva
Switzerland

Dear Sirs,

I recently inherited my grandfather's estate and found some items which
may be of some value.

Among the usual musty old paintings, I came across an insect collection
from his expedition across the Andes in 1924, including the following
rare species: a three-winged toad-eating nauga, a humpback dwizzle, six
leering mambo beetles in mating positions, and a multi-breasted stink
bug.

In addition, in a delicate glass container, I found a soup spoon
engraved "From B.J." Although it is possible that this was given to him
by his third wife, née Bertha Johansson, I have good reason to believe
that this spoon was a personal gift from Benito Juarez, the President
of Mexico.

Do you have a special department handling auctions of bugs and/or
presidential spoons? It would be great to make a lot of money by
selling this stuff. I look forward to your reply.

Yours sincerely,

[signature]

Habsburg, Feldman S.A.

FINE ART AUCTIONEERS

Mr. James C. Wade III
Montchoisi
1000 LAUSANNE 19

Geneva, January 11th 1990

Dear Mr. Wade,

Thank you for your letter of January 6th concerning the items you inherited from your grandfather's estate.

We regret to have to inform you that we could not deal with your collection as we do not sell such items.

May I take the liberty however to suggest that, if you have not already done so, you contact either Christie's or Sotheby's here in Geneva to enquire if they could deal with such a collection.

Thanking you for you kind interest in our company we remain at your disposition for any further information.

Yours sincerely,

Susan Ann Jones

202, route du Grand-Lancy, P.O. Box 125, CH-1213 Onex, Geneva, Switzerland
Tel. 022 57 25 30 - Telex 422 757 HF SA CH - Telefax 022 57 64 98
Incorporating Antiquorum and David Feldman S.A.

JAMES C. WADE III

Case postale 103
Montchoisi
1000 Lausanne 19
Switzerland

July 6, 1990

Bündnerstube Restaurant
Attn: The Manager
Carlton Elite Hotel
Nüschelerstrasse 1
8001 Zürich
Switzerland

Dear Sir,

I am writing a book on European cooking for overweight Americans, and I
wonder if you would be so kind as to help me with some information on
the section I will be devoting to great Swiss cuisine. I anticipate a
chapter of 3 or 4 pages.

Fondue is probably Switzerland's best-known contribution to the world's
cooking. I would like to know a little more about this famous dish. In
which region of Switzerland do the best fondue beans grow? Are beans
harvested late in any way preferable to younger, riper beans?

Second, where do you Swiss rank tomatoes along the fruit-vegetable
spectrum (1 = fruit, 10 = vegetable)?

Thank you very much for your kind assistance. I look forward very much
to your reply to the above address.

Yours sincerely,

James Wade

JAMES C. WADE III

Case postale 103
Montchoisi
1000 Lausanne 19
Switzerland

August 2, 1990

Bündnerstube Restaurant
Attn: The Manager
Carlton Elite Hotel
Nüschelerstrasse 1
8001 Zürich
Switzerland

Dear Sir,

About a month ago I wrote to you with some questions about Swiss
cooking in order to gain some insights for a book I am writing,
tentatively entitled *Smothered in Tripe* by Meniscus Lanugo (my pen-
name).

I have not heard from you and I wondered if I might respectfully ask
you please to respond, as my publisher, Wombat Books and Records of
Minnesota, has requested me to furnish them with a finished manuscript
soon or return their $15,000 travel advance.

I enclose a copy of my earlier letter, in case it escaped your
attention. Many thanks.

Yours sincerely,

Carlton Elite Hotel · Zürich

Herrn
James C. Wade III
Case postale lo3
Montchoisi

1ooo <u>Lausanne 19</u>

Zürich, 7. August 1990

Dear Mr. Wade

Thank you for your letter of August 2.

I am sorry not having been able to answer you before today
as I never received your first letter.

I have made you a photostatic copy of a little cookbook which
gives you two recipies of the tradional cheese fondue. In fact
it is better not to take too young cheese for the fondue.

What the tomatoes are concerned you would say that in Switzerland they are rated as vegetables and not as fruits.

I hope I have answered your questions to your satisfaction and
remain,

Yours sincerely,
CARLTON ELITE HOTEL

Edoardo Crivelli

147

JAMES C. WADE III

Case postale 103
Montchoisi
1000 Lausanne 19
Switzerland

January 10, 1990

Fortnum & Mason
Picadilly
London W1
England

Dear Sirs,

Recently I discovered the pleasures of one of France's little-known
delicacies, a drink called "jus des morpions." Its taste reminded me of
New England maple syrup, only crunchier.

At the time of my first tasting this rare juice, I had no idea what a
"morpion" is. However, having had the opportunity to consult a large
unabridged French-English dictionary, I have since discovered that a
"morpion" is some kind of crab louse. Lord knows how anyone came upon
the idea of squeezing juice from a crab louse, but the French, of
course, will eat just about anything that walks, crawls, oozes, or just
metabolizes.

At any rate, the juice of these little bugs is quite a stimulating
beverage, and I would like to stock up for special occasions.
Unfortunately, I have not been able to find it anywhere in Switzerland
or nearby France, and I haven't been able to locate the manufacturer of
the brand I tried, "Madame Fanny's."

Can you help me? If you carry this delectable juice yourselves, I would
like to order six of the handy one-gallon jugs. Otherwise I would
appreciate your letting me know, if possible, where I can find Madame
Fanny and her delightful parasites.

I look forward to your reply. Many thanks in the meantime.

Yours sincerely,

[signature]

FORTNUM & MASON PLC

PICCADILLY · LONDON
W1A 1ER

FACSIMILE 01-437 3278
TELEX 21160

TELEPHONE:
01-734 8040

Our Ref: ES/KM/

23 January 1990

James C Wade III
Case Postale 103, Montchoisi
1000 Lausanne 19
SWITZERLAND

Dear Sir

We write with reference to your letter dated 10 January 1990.

Unfortunately we do not stock "Madame Fanny's Jus des Morpions".

We regret we are unable to be of more assistance in this matter.

Yours faithfully

E SCHMITT

Section Head Central Order Department

REGISTERED IN ENGLAND
No. 84909

REGISTERED OFFICE: 181 PICCADILLY
LONDON W1A 1ER

JAMES C. WADE III

Case postale 103
Montchoisi
1000 Lausanne 19
Switzerland

August 2, 1990

Kitchener Sporting Goods
Aarbergerstrasse 40
3011 Bern
Switzerland

Re: Walumpa equipment

Dear Sirs,

I have been looking all over Switzerland for a walumpa racket and
wonder if you might have one for sale. Normally I play with a 32" as my
bilker is relatively long and I like a fast game. I would be interested
in buying one with a graphite fibble-stop if the price is right. For my
game, the best brand might well be the Zlad 6000.

Also, can you please quote me your price for 35 lbs. of tennis balls?

Thank you in advance for your reply.

Sincerely,

S P O R T I N G O O D S

BY KITCHENER

AARBERGERGASSE 40 3011 BERN (SCHWEIZ)   TELEFON: 031 222 333   FAX: 031 22 23 51

Mr. James C. Wade III
Case postale 103
Montchoisi
1000 Lausanne 19

Bern, 3.8.1990

Dear Mr. Wade,

Thank you for your letter dated August 2nd.

We feel sorry not be able to help you in this matter, but we d'ont handling Tennis equipments.

Hoping you will be more sucessful elsewhere, we remain,

with kind regards

KITCHENER SPORTING GOODS

B. Fankhauser

J.&E.HUBER H.MISCHLER

BANKVERBINDUNGEN: SCHWEIZ. BANKGESELLSCHAFT UND SCHWEIZ. BANKVEREIN BERN

JAMES C. WADE III

Case postale 103
Montchoisi
1000 Lausanne 19
Switzerland

February 19, 1990

Uppsala University
Department of Biology
P.O. Box 256
S - 751 05 Uppsala
Sweden

Dear Sirs,

I have a personal problem which I hope you can help me solve.

My wife and I just had a baby girl, and we are having trouble choosing
a name for our new daughter. We would both like to name her after
something from nature, but we just can't find anything suitable.

I personally like the name "Euglena" after an aunt on my mother's side,
but last night my wife pulled out a dictionary and showed me that this
word is actually the name for a freshwater protozoan algae. Her
favorite was "Melanoma," but that turns out to be something a doctor
ought to remove.

All the names we've liked have turned out to be fossil crustaceans,
reproductive organs, or diseases. Somehow I would feel bad if my
daughter went through life bearing the name of some arthropod's butt,
wouldn't you? Could you please suggest something we might be able to
live with?

Thank you so much for your help.

Yours sincerely,

James Wade

UPPSALA UNIVERSITY
Faculty of Natural Sciences
Section of Biology
Marita Wigren-Svensson

James C. Wade III
Case postale 103
Montchoisi
1000 Lausanne 19
SWITZERLAND

1 March 1990

Dear Mr Wade,

Thank you for your letter concerning a nice-sounding "natural" name for your baby girl.

You have been thinking about names as Euglena and Melanoma, but dropped the idea. I do agree that these names are not so well fitting on a beautiful little girl, since they stand for a flagellate and and a disese.

I would like to suggest you to choose one of following names:
a) From the plant kingdom
    Linnea - Linneaus favorite plant, a wonderful little flower
    Pyrola - a tiny but beautiful flower growing in the forest
    Flora - does not need explanation, does it?
b) From the animal kingdom
    Adalia - a ladybird with ten prickles
    Aromia - a metal coloured good smelling little beetle
    Bombina - a rare frog
    Cordulia - a beautiful dragon fly
    Perla - a mayfly living near rivers

Why not name the little girl **Linnea Adalia** or **Perla Pyrola**? Please let us know what you decide!

Yours sincerely,

Marita Wigren-Svensson
Marita Wigren-Svensson
Director of Studies

JAMES C. WADE III

Case postale 103
Montchoisi
1000 Lausanne 19
Switzerland

March 12, 1990

Uppsala University
Attn: Marita Wigren-Svensson
Faculty of Natural Sciences
Section of Biology
P.O. Box 256
S - 751 05 Uppsala
Sweden

Dear Ms. Wigren-Svensson,

Thank you very much for your letter of March 1 with the suggestions of
plant and animal kingdom names for our baby daughter. They were all
very beautiful, especially Bombina, the frog. Unfortunately, however,
this is a better description of my wife than of our little girl.

After much soul-searching, we have decided to call our daughter "Tibia
Fibula Wade" after her cute legs. I am sure that if you could see her,
you would agree that this name suits her very well.

Thanks again for all the trouble you went to. We will keep the list
handy for future babies.

Yours sincerely,

154

JAMES C. WADE III

P.O. Box 103
Montchoisi
1000 Lausanne 19
Switzerland

July 31, 1990

La Salle University
Maneville, Louisiana 70470-4000
USA

Dear Sirs,

I saw your recent ad in the *International Herald Tribune* and would be
very interested in converting my extensive life experience into a
college degree.

Personal data: I am 42 years old and have no formal education beyond
law school. My professional experience has been in ranching, human
organ trading (a very brief stint), classical guitar, and
mergers'n'acquisitions.

I'm sure that my life has been good enough to count for at least a
dental degree. My second choice would be a Masters in Oriental
Literature.

I look forward to hearing from you with some suggestions on how I can
best proceed. In the meantime, thanks in advance for your reply.

Yours sincerely,

PS. I played a lot of ball in high school and would particularly like
to know if I can apply any of my hoops experience to an athletic
scholarship at La Salle.

155

UNIVERSITY

Aug 6, 1990

JAMES WADE, III
PO BOX 103
MONTCHOISI
1000 LAUSANNE 19 SWITZERLAND

RE: Credentialization, Work Experience, & Prior Academic Credit

Dear JAMES,

Thank you for your interest in LaSalle University. We have
enclosed a LaSalle Catalog Tape and Information Packet, which
includes a portfolio evaluation data form.

Please complete the portfolio evaluation form in as much detail
as possible, and please enclose any and all documentation which
you deem relevant.

LaSalle's approach to each student is individualized and
personalized and we will be pleased to spend as much time as
necessary to answer any and all questions, about our educational
programs, and your individual evaluation.

For students outside the U.S. we have found the fastest method is
either to call us at 504-624-8932, or to use our international
fax line, 504-624-8931. Both the international line and the fax,
are operational 24 hours a day, seven days a week.

If you have any questions, please do not hesitate to contact a
member of the administrative staff at any time.

Sincerely,

Gina Cavaretta
Admissions Coordinator

JAMES C. WADE III

P.O. Box 103
Montchoisi
1000 Lausanne 19
Switzerland

August 13, 1990

La Salle University
Attn: Gina Cavaretta
Admissions Coordinator
Mandeville, Louisiana 70470-4000
USA

Dear Gina,

Many thanks for your individualized and personalized letter and the brochure describing your degree programs. The School of Theocentric Counseling looks like it could be the answer to my needs.

Financial assistance is going to be important for me. Before I fill in the Life Experience questionnaire and send you the $55 evaluation fee, I really need to know whether I have any chance of being accepted on a full basketball scholarship at La Salle.

What would be the best way for you to evaluate my basketball experience? If it would help, I suppose I could get an affidavit from one of my old coaches. The head coach knew me best, but unfortunately he died a few years ago in a freak bowling accident. Would you please let me know whether I should contact one of the assistant coaches and have him start working on a reference? I'd like to get all these financial matters settled as soon as possible.

Thank you for considering my special questions. I am looking forward to hearing from you soon.

Yours,

[signature]

JAMES C. WADE III

Case postale 103
Montchoisi
1000 Lausanne 19
Switzerland

March 23, 1990

Galerie Koller,
Antique Dealers
Rue Athenée 2
1206 Geneva
Switzerland

Dear Sirs,

I have just inherited some interesting antique furniture from a
relative in England, and I would like to know more about one or two
unusual pieces. Perhaps with your specialized knowledge you could give
me some idea whether these pieces have any particular value.

The first is a Georgian cleaf-shouldered foncet, with brass tharns on
each side. There is a small twistle in the center of the ballop, up at
the top edge of the grimmet, and each of the legs has a fransette at
the end. The wood is mahogany and the overall condition is excellent.

The other piece is a wing-back, adaman-type westercloggin which appears
to me to be Queen Anne in style. Over the bastrick on the left side are
the initials J.B.M. and all around the outer whittings there is a
continuously carved hanticle. It is also made of very dark wood and is
quite a handsome piece.

Have you encountered any such pieces here in Switzerland? If so I would
be particularly grateful if you could give me a rough idea how much
they might be worth, if I were to sell them.

Thank you for your help in this matter. I look forward to hearing from
you.

Yours sincerely,

James Wade

GALERIE KOLLER
BUREAU DE GENÈVE

2, RUE DE L'ATHÉNÉE

1205 GENÈVE

TÉLÉPHONE :

DE SUISSE 022/21 03 85

DE FRANCE 19-41/22-21 03 85

FAX : 022/28 78 72

RELATION BANCAIRE :

CRÉDIT SUISSE

Mr. James C. Wade III
Case Postale 103
Montchoisi

1000 <u>Lausanne</u> 19

1205 GENÈVE March 27 1990

Dear Mr. Wade,

We have received your letter of March 23, and thank you for your interest in our company. Unfortunately, it is very difficult to give you an idea of the value of your pieces based on descriptions. If you have occaision to send us a photograph of each piece concerned, along with their dimensions, we would be able to provide you with an estimated auction value.

Thank you once again for your consideration, and we look forward to hearing from you soon.

Sincerely,

Karl Green

Karl Green
Galerie Koller Genève

SIÈGE SOCIAL DE LA GALERIE KOLLER S.A., RÄMISTRASSE 8, 8024 ZURICH

JAMES C. WADE III

Case postale 103
Montchoisi
1000 Lausanne 19
Switzerland

April 4, 1990

Galerie Koller,
Antique Dealers
Attn: Mr. Karl Green
Rue Athenée 2
1206 Geneva
Switzerland

Dear Mr. Green,

Thank you for your letter of March 27 regarding my foncet and westercloggin.

I was just about to take photos of these two pieces, as you suggested, when they were both crushed under another antique of mine, a 300-lb. quaince-topped scriblin from the Restoration period, which fell over on top of them thanks to some indoor antics of my dog, a rather nasty poodle named Lothar.

As this furniture is now junk, I have sold it as firewood.

Many thanks for your readiness to help me.

Your sincerely,

James Wade

JAMES C. WADE III

P.O. Box 103
Montchoisi
1000 Lausanne 19
Switzerland

April 6, 1990

Collectors News Magazine
Attn: The Editor
Box 156
Grundy Center, Iowa   50638
USA

Dear Sirs,

I have inherited a mint condition copy of the very first issue of *Big Glands* magazine (December 1955), and I wondered if you could tell me how much it is worth on the market.

This is the issue containing the famous 6-page spread on Mamie Eisenhower.

Thank you in advance for your reply.

Yours sincerely,

[signature]

COLLECTORS NEWS & THE ANTIQUE REPORTER

506 SECOND STREET • P.O. BOX 156
GRUNDY CENTER, IA 50638-0156

PHONE (319) 824-5456
FAX 319-824-3414

April 25, 1990

James C. Wade III
P.O. Box 103
Montchoisi
1000 Lausanne 19
Switzerland

Dear James:

Regarding the value of your first issue <u>Big</u> <u>Glands</u> magazine:

I have not found a reference to this particular magazine in any of the price guides specializing in paper collectibles. This would indicate that the magazine is not widely traded.

Generally the value of such obscure items as yours lies in the collectors themselves. Should you find another collector who really wants your issue the value will increase. However, without any activity of such an item recorded in our marketplace I cannot state a suggest value.

Yours for collecting,

Linda Kruger
Editor

162

JAMES C. WADE III

P.O. Box 103
Montchoisi
1000 Lausanne 19
Switzerland

January 15, 1990

Best Western Kings Row Inn
Attn: The Manager
4200 State Line Ave.
Texarkana, Arkansas 75502
USA

Dear Sir,

A couple of months ago I was staying at your hotel and I believe I
mislaid a pair of cufflinks in your lounge.

They are gold-plated, about three inches long, and bear an inscription in
inlaid rubies that says "Mongol Empire 1211-1502."

I am fairly sure that I left them in the cocktail lounge, where, if my
memory serves, you were featuring Kenny Kaye and his Vocal Stylings.
During a break, one of the Vocal Stylings joined me for a drink at my
table and as she was admiring my cufflinks, I took them off so she could
have a better look.

By any chance have they turned up? They have a lot of sentimental value,
because they were personally presented to me by Richard Nixon.

Looking forward to hearing from you soon.

Yours sincerely,

JAMES C. WADE III

P.O. Box 103
Montchoisi
1000 Lausanne 19
Switzerland

March 9, 1990

Best Western Kings Row Inn
Attn: The Manager
4200 State Line Ave.
Texarkana, Arkansas 75502
USA

Dear Sir,

In January of this year I wrote asking if some cufflinks I lost in your
hotel might have been found. They are pretty easy to spot since they
are big and gold and inscribed with the dates of the rise and fall of
the Mongol Empire (1211-1502, although some historians place this
later).

So far I have not heard from you, and I was hoping against hope you
might have come up with them in the meantime. I would hate to lose them
because Former President Richard Milhous Nixon gave them to me after he
trounced me in a game of racquetball in Vancouver in 1971.

Of course it's possible it was another Best Western hotel altogether.
I've stayed in just about all of them and I have a hard time keeping
them apart in my mind. Could you maybe check around at the other ones
for me?

Thanks for your help.

Yours,

James Wade

March 19, 1990

James C. Wade
Montchoisi
1000 Lausanne 19
Switzerland

Dear Mr. Wade:

We replied to your first letter, but its apparent you
did not receive it. We searched the room after your
first alert and found no cufflinks.

I'm sorry you lost them, as I realize the sentimental
value. I voted for Mr. Nixon.

Yours truly,

E. M. Jones, Sr.
Owner
Kings Row Inns of America

"Catering to the Commercial Traveler"

JAMES C. WADE III

P.O. Box 103
Montchoisi
1000 Lausanne 19
Switzerland

May 4, 1990

National Center for Health Statistics
3700 East-West Highway
Hyattsville, Maryland 20782
USA

Dear Sirs,

Could you please furnish me with the number of U.S. hospital admissions
in 1988 (or the latest year available) for foreign objects lodged
within the nose?

As for the foreign object, I would like a breakdown as follows:

a. Lima beans, baked beans, peas, nuts'n'raisins, potato chips, and
French fries.

b. Inanimate, naturally occurring objects such as rocks, sticks, pieces
of bark, hunks of dirt, etc.

c. Manmade objects such as ballpoint pens, marbles, forks, paper clips,
staples, thumbtacks, etc.

d. Non-solid objects such as shaving cream, peanut butter (smooth only,
not crunchy), Jell-O, and so forth.

Thank you very much for helping me with my research. I look forward to
hearing from you.

Yours sincerely,

James Wade

DEPARTMENT OF HEALTH & HUMAN SERVICES

Public Health Service
Centers for Disease Control

National Center for Health Statistics
3700 East-West Highway
Hyattsville, MD 20782

May 31, 1990

James C. Wade III
P. O. Box 103
Montchoisi
1000 Lausanne 19
Switzerland

Dear Mr. Wade:

This is in reference to your inquiry to the National Center for Health Statistics (NCHS) regarding information on foreign objects lodged within the nose.

NCHS conducts an annual survey which has the capability of providing statistics in this area. This survey, the National Hospital Discharge Survey (NHDS), collects statistical data on conditions diagnosed and surgical and nonsurgical procedures performed in non-Federal short-stay hospitals. Data are obtained from hospital records.

The recording of foreign objects lodged within the nose is in category E912 of the International Classification of Diseases, 9th Revision, Clinical Modification, Third Edition, Volume I. Included in this category also are aspiration and inhalation of foreign body except food (into respiratory tract) NOS, obstruction of pharynx by foreign body, compression, interruption of respiration and obstruction of respiration by foreign body in esophagus. In 1988, the latest data year available, the NHDS did not observe enough diagnoses for a reliable estimate. This has been indicative of this category for the past several years.

Please let me know if I can assist you further.

Sincerely

Linda R. Washington
Public Affairs Specialist

167

JAMES C. WADE III

P.O. Box 103
Montchoisi
1000 Lausanne 19
Switzerland

December 2, 1989

Marine Mammal Commission
Attn: Mr. John R. Twiss, Jr.
Executive Director
1625 Eye Street N.W.
Washington, DC 20006
USA

Dear Mr. Twiss,

About a week ago I was strolling along the bank of the Lake of Thun not
far from Interlaken when I spotted a 10-foot manatee basking just below
the surface of a calm, shallow part of the lake.

I reported this sighting to the police, who referred me to a special
Bureau at Interlaken City Hall. There a Mrs. Scmutzli told me that
there had been many recent sightings of American animals in the area,
including a pronghorn antelope, two armadillos, a wolverine, Bigfoot,
and a star-nosed mole.

Furthermore, she said that as an American citizen, I am required to
report all such sightings to U.S. authorities. After looking up
"manatee" in a huge reference book, she gave me your name and address.

Mr. Twiss, I am confused about the proper procedure in a case like this
and wonder if you could advise me as a U.S. taxpayer exactly what you
do with this information.

Thank you in advance for taking the time to consider this matter.

Yours sincerely,

[signature]

MARINE MAMMAL COMMISSION
1625 EYE STREET, N.W.
WASHINGTON, DC 20006

December 19, 1989

Mr. James C. Wade III
Post Office Box 103
Montchoisi
1000 Lausanne 19
Switzerland

Dear Mr. Wade:

Many thanks for your letter of 2 December 1989. It arrived on the 11th.

I am perplexed by your report. I do not think that a manatee could survive in the Lake of Thun. The water temperatures are too cold. As you may or may not know, high numbers of manatees have died during exceptionally cold periods in Florida. Although I do not have hard data on which to base this, my guess is that water temperatures in the Lake of Thun in January and February would be far below any ever experienced in Florida. Therefore, I think this must be an animal of another species.

It was kind of you to have taken the trouble to do the research to find the name of the Commission and my name. I am grateful to you and wish that I could be of more help.

Sincerely,

John R. Twiss, Jr.
Executive Director

169

JAMES C. WADE III

Case postale 103
Montchoisi
1000 Lausanne 19
Switzerland

December 2, 1989

The British Museum
Attn: New Exhibits Director
Great Russell Street
London WC1B 3DG
England

Dear Sirs,

Thanks to the foresight of my great aunt, I own Hermann Goering's
toothbrush. Would you be interested in exhibiting it?

I thank you in advance for your reply.

Yours sincerely,

PS. I might also be able to arrange a donation of Tutankhamen's pocket
comb.

The British Museum

London WC1B 3DG

Telephone 01-636 1555 ext.

James C Wade III
Case Postale 103
Montchoisi
1000 Lausanne 19
Switzerland

Your reference

Our reference

Date 11 December 1989

Dear Mr Wade,

Thank you for your letter of 2 December.

I congratulate you on the foresight of your great
aunt in securing Hermann Goering's toothbrush but
I regret that this kind of item does not fall
within the scope of our collections.

An Egyptian 'pocket' comb might well be relevant
to us, but if it came from the tomb of Tutankhamun
it should go to the Egyptian Museum in Cairo.

However it occurs to me to add that were you to
come across the treasure of King John we would be
interested.

Yours sincerely,

Geoffrey House
Head of Public Services

Inland and Overseas Telegrams: Britishmus London WC1

JAMES C. WADE III

Case postale 103
Montchoisi
1000 Lausanne 19
Switzerland

December 18, 1989

The British Museum
Attn: Mr Geoffrey House
Head of Public Services
Great Russell Street
London WC1B 3DG
England

Dear Mr. House,

Thank you for your letter to me dated December 11. Although I would
love to take the credit for my great aunt's farsightedness in securing
various toilet articles from great men in history, I'm afraid I can't
do so. I am only sorry that they will not enter your collections.

As for Tutankhamen's pocket comb, I must admit that it did not come
directly from his tomb but rather from a "Great Pyramid Sale" in
Martinsville, Indiana; however, the salesman vouched for its
authenticity. It cost twelve dollars. Do you think I ought to get in
touch with Cairo?

Thanks for the tip about King John. The attic is full of old stuff, and
I shall keep an eye out for anything that looks like it might be his.

Merry Christmas!

[signature]

PS. How *did* Tut spell his name anyway?

The British Museum

London WC1B 3DG

Telephone 01-636 1555 ext.

Tutankhamun

James C Wade III
Case Postale 103
Montchoisi
1000 Lausanne 19
Switzerland

Your re[f]

Our reference

Date 22 January 1990

Dear Mr Wade,

Thank you for your letter of 18 December.

The news that the Tutankhamun pocket comb which you
mentioned was included in a 'Great Pyramid Sale' in
Indiana suggests caution, and I recommend you get
someone who knows about ancient Egyptian artefacts to
look at it.

I enclose a version of Tutankhamun's name in
hieroglyphs. Those at the top are usually translated
as the titles 'King of Upper and Lower Egypt' and
'Son of Re' while the oval cartouches below contain
his name.

It occurs to me that you may enjoy visiting our
forthcoming exhibition "Fake? The Art of Deception"
(9 March - 2 September). My two favourite objects
to be included are a furry trout and a merman.

Yours sincerely,

Geoffrey House
Head of Public Services

Inland and Overseas Telegrams: Britishmus London WC1

JAMES C. WADE III

P.O. Box 103
Montchoisi
1000 Lausanne 19
Switzerland

December 6, 1990

Girard
1810 Rittenhouse Square
Apt. 1705
Philadelphia, Pennsylvania 19103
USA

Dear Girard,

I saw your ad in *The Progressive* and felt compelled to write. Even though I myself was not the subject of a behavior control experiment, I am sure that I witnessed a particularly diabolical one, on a massive scale.

In 1983 I was working as a food mechanic in Stockholm as part of my Ph.D. degree program in fruit sciences. One of my colleagues, a fellow doctoral candidate from Wisconsin, told me one evening of a plan he had worked out "with U.S. government backing" which would allow his grant supervisors the opportunity to study human behavior modification under the influence of so-called "fiber laxatives" which would be administered to dozens of people in some kind of a fruit soup.

The actual ingredients were supplied to him by contacts he said he had at the American Embassy. About a week later, the soup was served to 200 members of the Royal Pay-Telephone Society at a banquet they were holding in honor of the invention of a new kind of coin slot. I was not present but I was told that everyone who ate the soup rushed out into the snow, shrieking and flapping their arms like birds. Apparently someone from the Embassy filmed the entire event from behind a mirror.

Although I can't be certain who was behind this, I felt sure that you would want to hear about it.

Sincerely,

James Wade

December 14, 1990.

Dear Mr Wade,

     Thank you very much for your recent letter. The
information will be put to good use.

     Lausanne is a most beautiful city. I have spent
some time there during happier days.

     I have a friend in the Swiss foreign service, in
case it becomes necessary for you to seek protection.
He is familiar with the work I am doing, bringing
American Nazis to justice. His name is ALEXANDER WITTWER.
He lives in Bern, when he is not posted overseas.

     I expect to be returning to Europe some time this
coming year, though progress here has become very rapid.
I will surely call, and hope to arrange a meeting with
you.

                         Very truly yours,

                         Harlan Girard

JAMES C. WADE III

Case postale 103
Montchoisi
1000 Lausanne 19
Switzerland

February 18, 1990

Presleymania Records
Hofwiesenstrasse 285
8050 Zürich
Switzerland

Dear Sirs,

I have been an Elvis fan since forever. Imagine my excitement when I discovered that your shop exists.

For a long time, I have been trying to find a copy of one of Elvis' rarities. Of course I'm referring to his immortal "Belch for me, Baby," which he recorded in Memphis for the Sputum Label in 1955. Do you by chance have this in stock?

Many thanks in advance.

Yours sincerely,

GRACE GASSER
RENNWEG 9
6700 KÜSNACHT
SWITZERLAND
TEL. 01 911 05 05

26. FEBRUARY 1990

HI!

MY NAME IS GRACE GASSER, AND I AM WRITING TO IN ANSWER TO YOUR LETTER TO
MICHAEL DIETHELM OF PRESLEYMANIA RECORDS. AS MICHAEL DOESN'T SPEAK ENGLISH,
AND I WAS BORN IN ENGLAND, I HAVE OFFERED TO ANSWER YOUR LETTER.

LIKE YOU I HAVE BEEN AN ELVIS FAN SINCE FOREVER. YOUR ENQUIRY ABOUT AN ELVIS
VERSION OF "BELCH FOR ME, BABY" ON SPUTUM LABEL WOULD CERTAINLY BE A SENSATION
IF IT EXISTED. AS A LONGTIME ELVIS FAN, I HAVE NEVER EVEN HEARD OF THE SONG OR THE
LABEL. MAYBE YOU HAVE A VERSION OF THIS SONG FROM SOMEONE ELSE.

ARE YOU SURE THAT THIS ISN'T A JOKE? I DOUBT VERY MUCH THAT YOU COULD PRODUCE
ANY KIND OF EVIDENCE THAT THIS RECORDING EVER EXISTED, BUT IF YOU CAN, THEN PLEASE
DO SO, AND ALLOW THE REST OF THE ELVIS FANS IN THIS WORLD TO SHARE YOUR
DISCOVERY.

AS AN ELVIS FAN YOU WILL PROBABLY BE INTERESTED IN ELVIS MEETING AND SO I ENCLOSE
AN INVITATION TO MY OPEN HOUSE FOR ELVIS FANS ON 31. MARCH. PRESLEYMANIA WILL
BE BRINGING RECORDS FOR SALE AND YOU WOULD HAVE AN OPPORTUNITY TO POSSIBLY FIND
SOME OTHER ELVIS RARITY. YOU WOULD ALSO BE ABLE TO MEET A NUMBER OF LONGTIME ELVIS
FANS.

SO MAYBE WE'LL SEE YOU THERE. I LOOK FORWARD TO EITHER MEETING YOU, OR HEARING FROM
YOU WITH REGARD TO THIS STRANGE RECORDING YOU ARE LOOKING FOR.

YOURS SINCERELY

Grace

JAMES C. WADE III

P.O. Box 103
Montchoisi
1000 Lausanne 19
Switzerland

March 3, 1990

Ms. Grace Gasser
Rennweg 3
8700 Küsnacht
Switzerland

Howdy Ma'am,

Thanks so kindly for your letter. It is always good to know another
Elvis fan.

I wish I could prove that "Belch for me, Baby" really existed, but how
can I? The company had only shipped three dozen copies before Sputum
Records' only studio and warehouse were destroyed in a freak avalanche.
I'm surprised you never heard of it. I guess in Europe you missed out
on a lot of interesting news like this.

Thank you for the invitation to your Elvis Open House. I will try to
make it, although I am sort of committed to going to my sister's
wedding that weekend. If I can get out of it, then I'll see you at the
party.

In any case I am interested in hearing if any of your friends have seen
Elvis recently. Personally I do not believe in all those UFO stories.
Friends of mine say they have seen him working at a Kentucky Fried
Chicken in Guam. I'd sure appreciate an update if anybody can offer
one.

Yours,

[signature]

PS. How can anybody enjoy Elvis without knowing any English?!

JAMES C. WADE III

Case postale 103
Montchoisi
1000 Lausanne 19
Switzerland

February 18, 1990

Chairman
Department of History
University of Hamburg
2000 Hamburg 13
Federal Republic of Germany

Dear Sir,

I am preparing a biography of Otto von Bismarck for publication late
next year. I wonder if you could please confirm for me from the
available records that he had seven toes on each foot and was brought
up speaking fluent Korean?

Thank you very much in advance for helping me with this most important
research.

Yours sincerely,

[signature]

JAMES C. WADE III

Case postale 103
Montchoisi
1000 Lausanne 19
Switzerland

June 29, 1990

Chairman
Department of History
University of Hamburg
2000 Hamburg 13
Federal Republic of Germany

Dear Sir,

Several weeks ago I wrote to your department at the university with an
enquiry about the number of Otto von Bismarck's toes: ten or fourteen?

My assumption is based partly on Bismarck's own diary, in which he
often counts all his appendages, coming up with a total of 31. I have
accounted for all but four, and must therefore surmise that the Iron
Chancellor was endowed with extra toes.

By the way, I have determined in the meantime that Bismarck was raised
speaking *German*, not Korean, so you might want to put a note to that
effect in any books on him that might be in your library.

Looking forward to hearing from you.

Sincerely yours,

James Wade

PS. I am good for over twelve hundred dollars.

UNIVERSITÄT HAMBURG

HISTORISCHES SEMINAR

Prof. Dr. Kersten Krüger
Geschäftsführender Direktor

Historisches Seminar
Von-Melle-Park 6, IX, 2000 Hamburg 13

Herrn
James C. Wade III

Case postale 103
CH 1000 Lausanne
S c h w e i z

Fernsprecher: (040) 41 23 -   2585
Behördennetz: 9.38. („   ) } Durchwahl

Telex-Nr.: 214732 unihh d
Telefax-Nr.: national   (040) 4123-2449
             international (4940) 4123-2449

Datum und Zeichen Ihres Schreibens   Aktenzeichen (bei Antwort bitte angeben)   Datum

25. Juli 1990

Betreff

Dear Sir!

Thank you very much for your letter of june 29th, the only one we received from you. Your questions about Bismarck are most interesting, but unfortunately, we cannot give you definite answers.

Your remark about Bismarck's nationality is quite correct: he was a German and not a Korean.

As to the numbers of Bismarck's toes we cannot give any definite information. As most human beings, we suppose he had ten. Maybe that the number of toes had influence on Bismarck's politics, but until now there is no evidence for this interesting presumption.

Further information you will easily get from the new and very good biography:

Lothar Gall: Bismarck. Der weisse Revolutionär. Frankfurt 3d ed. 1980.

Yours sincerely

181

JAMES C. WADE III

P.O. Box 103
Montchoisi
1000 Lausanne 19
Switzerland

April 17, 1990

Rossweid Animal Clinic
Attn: Dr Peter Attinger, Dr. Vet. Med.
Rossweidstrasse 1
Gockhausen
8044 Zürich
Switzerland

Dear Dr. Attinger,

Would you perform a nose reconstruction for my dog? I have never been
completely satisfied with his profile and think that he would look much
better, and benefit from the added utility, if he could be given a
prehensile nose, or even a full trunk. Preferably this would be about
two feet long in order to reach the ground and assist him in bringing
me my slippers, the newspaper, etc.

I look forward to hearing from you soon.

Yours sincerely,

[signature]